SLIMMING COOKBOOK

Joy Leslie Gibson

First published in 1982 by
Octopus Books Limited
59 Grosvenor Street, London W1

Third impression, 1983

© 1982 Hennerwood Publications Limited

ISBN 0 906320 91 7

Produced by Mandarin Publishers Limited
Printed in Hong Kong

NOTES

1. All recipes serve four unless otherwise stated.

2. All spoon measurements are level.

3. All eggs are sizes 3 and 4 unless otherwise stated.

4. Preparation times given are an average calculated during recipe testing.

5. Metric and imperial measurements have been calculated separately. Use one set of measurements only as they are not exact equivalents.

6. Cooking times may vary slightly depending on the individual oven. Dishes should be placed in the centre of the oven unless otherwise specified.

7. Always preheat the oven or grill to the specified temperature.

8. All sugar is granulated unless otherwise stated.

9. Spoon measures can be bought in both imperial and metric sizes to give accurate measurement of small quantities.

ACKNOWLEDGEMENTS

Photography: Robert Golden
Photographic styling: Antonia Gaunt
Preparation of food for photography:
Mary Cadogan

The publishers would like to thank the following companies for the loan of props for photography:

Circa, 14 Sloane Street, London SW1

The Conran Shop, 77-79 Fulham Road, London SW3

Treasure Island, 81 Pimlico Road, London SW1

CONTENTS

INTRODUCTION

If you are overweight you have a far greater chance of serious illness, such as heart attack, bronchial troubles, varicose veins and diabetes.

To assess your correct weight, check with the charts in this book and, if you feel it necessary, consult your doctor about the weight he thinks is a healthy one for you, then work out a varied diet for yourself with his approval. Always remember that a varied diet will not make you fat if you eat foods in the correct quantities. If you cook properly trying out different recipes, like the ones in this book, you won't get bored as you might well do living on just diet foods. When working out your eating plan, bear in mind that a balanced diet must include the following:

Protein: fish, meat, poultry, milk, eggs, cheese, beans, bread, pasta and rice.
Fats: butter, margarine, cheese, vegetable oils. You do need a little fat when on a diet to provide energy. Most people eat far too much fat and you can restrict yourself here quite easily. But beware, many foods contain hidden fat, particularly meat. If you restrict yourself to 15 g/½ oz butter or margarine a day, you will find this enough for your needs.
Vitamins: vitamins A, B, C, D, E and K are needed daily by the body for good health. A varied, healthy diet containing fruit, vegetables, fish, liver, eggs, meat and bread will supply sufficient amounts.
Minerals: minerals are also needed daily, especially calcium and iron. Calcium is found in milk, cheese, yogurt, sardines, salmon and green vegetables. Iron is found in liver, lean meat, eggs and dried fruit. Other minerals are needed in very small amounts and a varied, healthy diet will provide them.
Fibre: wholemeal bread, porridge, potato skins and green vegetables. Research is currently being carried out on the value of fibre (roughage) in the diet.

The following points cover briefly what causes obesity, how to get rid of it, how to eat well without putting on weight and how to keep to a healthy weight.

CAUSES OF WEIGHT GAIN

You put on weight when you eat more than you need for the life you lead. This doesn't always mean that you are greedy and eat to excess. As each individual varies – different shapes, different heights – the rate at which food is used up varies too. This is called the metabolic rate; some people use up their food more efficiently and economically than others, so those with a slower rate just have to eat less. Infuriating but true. You can no more help putting on weight than you can help the colour of your eyes. But you can stabilize your weight by eating sensibly.

WRITE IT DOWN

Most people who claim they eat very little, yet still put on weight, often don't know how much they eat or how many calories different foods contain. To help, get into the habit of writing down each day exactly what you eat and when. You may be surprised to find out that you nibble all day long – a biscuit with a cup of tea which has milk and sugar in it can add up to 630 kJ/150 calories; the odd bit of cheese you eat when you come back from work can add another 420 kJ/100 calories; the piece of cake you finished up so that it wouldn't be left is another 1045 kJ/250 calories; the croissant you had with a friend in the coffee shop added 1090 kJ/260 calories, plus another 330 kJ/80 calories for the butter! By the end of the day, you have eaten 2500 kJ/600 calories more than you needed. Cut out all those extras and you will lose a pound a week easily!

CALORIES EXPLAINED

A kilojoule or calorie is simply a name given to a unit of energy contained in food. Each food has a kJ/calorie count per 25 g/1 oz. So it follows that there are no actual fattening foods – all foods are *potentially* fattening, though some more so than others. Thus occur some of the myths of slimming. Pasta, bread and potatoes can easily be eaten by slimmers, providing that they don't go too mad and eat them only in moderate quantities. A 100 g/4 oz boiled potato contains about 420 kJ/100 calories; it makes you feel full and is therefore worth eating just for that property, provided your total daily calories are not exceeded. The same comment can be made about bread. About 25 g/1 oz bread is about 250 kJ/60 calories; bread contains many valuable nutrients, so you should eat 2–3 slices every day. Eat crispbread if you like it, but remember that about 3 slices of crispbread are equal in calorie value to a slice of bread, so if you lightly spread them with butter or margarine you are, in fact, probably consuming *more* calories than eating one slice of bread lightly spread with butter! 25 g/1 oz uncooked pasta (about 75 g/3 oz cooked) equals a slice of bread in calorie value, so sometimes substitute pasta for bread – it adds variety to your slimming regime and is no more fattening. Don't, of course, add a high calorie sauce with it – serve with fresh tomatoes or onions, herbs and a sprinkling of Parmesan.

MEDICAL PROBLEMS

Glandular trouble is often given as a reason for being overweight, but in fact only a very small percentage (some say as little as 2 per cent) of people really have medical problems that stop them losing weight. Consult your doctor.

Water retention may be a problem, especially for women: some women put on weight after going on the pill, so consult your doctor and if possible try a different pill that doesn't cause water retention. Alternatively, you will have to diet those several pounds away. All women retain water at certain times in their monthly cycle, but this is nothing to be alarmed at. Don't weigh yourself too often – the body can sometimes suddenly put on several pounds because of what you have eaten, but it disposes of this weight just as quickly. Most people weigh more at the end of the day than at the beginning. Weigh yourself once a week only – weight can vary from day to day. Some nutritionists believe that carbohydrates (rice, pasta, jams, sugar, cakes, bread, potatoes) can cause water retention.

COPING WITH HUNGER

There are people who suffer from emotional hunger – people who eat when upset, worried or bored. This is a difficult problem and one that can only be cured by persistent effort. It isn't *real* hunger; in these cases eating is a comfort. To help overcome this, keep a diary to see when you treat yourself to a comfort snack. If it is at a certain time or in a certain situation then once you have become aware of this, distract yourself at that time or don't get into that situation. For instance, if you come home from work hungry either don't get home at that time – go to an evening class, have a game of squash or even telephone a friend – thus avoiding going into the kitchen until it is time to prepare the evening meal. If you get bored in the middle of the afternoon sitting alone at home, then go out for a walk, go to a

museum, go to an adult education class or practise a craft that you enjoy over the danger period. Also, keep plenty of prepared salad vegetables so that if you *must* eat, you eat something of very low calorie value.

AVOIDING TEMPTATION

Most people hate to see other people succeed where they fail, so you won't get any help from them. Don't ever tell friends that you are dieting – it is boring and a sure signal for everyone to gang together to get you off it. When eating in a friend's house be careful how much and what you eat. Take a drink and put it down without drinking it; take the cake but don't eat it. It's quite easy really. Or say you are on a course of pills that forbids you eating cheese or whatever, or forbids you to drink alcohol. Get a sudden allergy to that drink or food. But never confess to dieting!

It is best to get your family on your side – explain to the children that you will be more able to join in with their fun if you are slimmer and healthier; that you want them to be proud of you (most children are embarrassed by fat parents) and ask them to eat their sweets and chocolates, crisps and biscuits in their own rooms, just to help you. Of course, you should really actively discourage them from eating too much of these foods so that they don't have the problems of fatness that you have. Never give children sweets as a reward, it sets up the cycle of going to food for comfort and getting fat, then going again to food for comfort, hating yourself, and eating again. And so getting fatter!

RETAINING IDEAL WEIGHT

It is a sad fact that once a fat person, always a fat person. So plan to find a way of eating that you can keep to for the rest of your life. Going on a diet then bingeing and returning to the diet is very bad for your health. The occasional binge in the middle of a regime of healthy eating is all right, but continually dieting and then bingeing is injurious.

DRINKING ON A DIET

Like every other food or drink, alcohol has a kJ/calorie count (about 290 kJ/70 calories for a small glass of wine). Alcohol does not provide much in the way of nourishment, so while you are actually losing weight it is better to cut it out if possible. Then when you have arrived at the weight you want to be, add it back gradually; but still be aware of the calorie count.

BREAKFAST

There is some evidence that eating breakfast helps to waken up your metabolism after a night's rest. The best argument for eating breakfast though is that you are less likely to nibble during the morning if you have something at the start of the day. If you really prefer to do without it, then make sure that your mid-morning snack is nutritious (a hard-boiled egg, 25 g/1 oz cheese, tomatoes) rather than a bun or biscuits.

CHEATING

If you know you are a cheat then legislate for it. Allocate a number of calories for your cheating if you must. But it is really better not to cheat – it makes you feel better. If you cheat too often there really is no point in trying to get slim. Don't look upon the diet as a punishment because it isn't; by trying to lose weight you are rewarding yourself with a more attractive body and a healthier way of life. Rewards are important, but they don't have to be rewards of food. Give yourself a treat every day: go to a play or film you want to see if you have succeeded in staying on your slimming regime for a week; make a long-distance call to a friend. Write down your daily treat and glow with satisfaction over it! Above all, remember that the only person you cheat when you slip up while on a diet is yourself. That is important for you are letting your own integrity suffer.

COOKING FOR THE FAMILY

The recipes in this book can be enjoyed by everyone, there is nothing faddy about them. If you are the fatty among a family of skinnies, just add more potatoes, bread, rice for them or give them bigger portions. You will get slim, they will stay the same.

EXERCISING

Exercise does burn up calories, so regular consistent exercise will help. But it has to be kept up. An hour's extra, fairly brisk walk each day, for example, will burn off a pound of weight a week.

RATE OF WEIGHT LOSS

Everybody loses weight at different rates – it is the difference in metabolic rate. A small steady loss, say 1 kg/2 lb a week, is better than a larger, quick loss. There is less strain on your system, you feel better and you're more likely to keep to the diet. Roughly speaking, you have to eat 14630 kJ/3,500 calories less to lose 0.5 kg/ 1 lb weight. At first you will probably lose more – this is mainly due to eating less carbohydrate and therefore losing water, not fat. If you have a lot of weight to lose, you will find that as your body gets used to less food, it will slow up the rate at which you lose weight. You may have to eat less calories, but only do this in consultation with your doctor, and never go below 3340 kJ/800 calories a day. This is the minimum calories you need; less than this is dangerous to health.

EATING WITH YOUR EYES

We eat with our eyes as well as with our mouths, so cheat your eyes. Use small plates so that they look overflowing and you won't feel deprived. Have small portions of lots of interesting foods. There are lots of recipes in this book which are 420 kJ/100 calories or less; have several of these if you like many courses. Remember, home-made clear soup is low in calories and filling, so start a meal with this (or a vegetable or chicken stock if you haven't time to make a real soup). Make interesting salads. And don't forget a low-calorie pudding.

COOKING FOR PLEASURE

Turn your interest in food from just feeding yourself with it to becoming a good cook. There is nothing more pleasurable than cooking a delicious meal for people. Providing you watch your calories, you gain pleasure from the look of food as well as its taste. Make sure you really savour what you eat, many fat people don't really *taste* food, as they eat far too quickly. Become involved with food in a sensible way, then your diet won't bore you and you'll enjoy food again.

HOW TO USE THIS BOOK

VERY IMPORTANT
If you are more than 3 kg/7 lb over weight you must consult your doctor before starting any weight reduction.

NOTE ON KJ/CALORIE COUNTS

All the recipes in this book serve four. The approximate kJ/calorie count given is for one quarter of the recipe, not for the whole dish. If you eat more than one quarter of the dish then you must count more calories. Ingredients must be weighed or again the kJ/calorie count will be different. Some recipes, e.g. cakes, carry a kJ/calorie count for the whole dish but this is clearly stated.

WHAT TO SELECT IN YOUR DAILY INTAKE

For a healthy way of eating include the following foods:
About 75-175 g/3-6 oz protein each day.
50 g/2 oz bread or 1 slice bread and either 100 g/4 oz cooked potato or 75 g/3 oz cooked pasta or rice (25 g/1 oz uncooked).
3 pieces of fruit.
At least 175 g/6 oz green vegetables.
600 ml/1 pint skimmed milk (skimmed milk contains all the nutrients of ordinary milk *minus* the fat).
Do not eat more than 7 eggs each week (they have a high cholesterol content).
Do not eat more than 175 g/6 oz cheese (other than cottage cheese) each week.

HOW TO WORK OUT THE NUMBER OF KJ/CALORIES

Start off by consuming 5000 kJ/1200 calories a day. For instance for breakfast, if you have ½ grapefruit, 1 boiled egg, 1 piece of toast with a scraping of butter or margarine, tea or coffee with skimmed milk then you have already used up about 630 kJ/150 calories. The rest of your skimmed milk allowance will add up to 630 kJ/150 calories and your two other pieces of fruit about 500 kJ/120 calories. Adding to this, a second slice of bread (250 kJ/60 calories), already 1610 kJ/400 calories will have been used. This leaves 3340 kJ/800 calories for lunch and evening meals. How you distribute this can be worked out as you like and according to your family eating habits. But it is better to have two smaller meals than a snack and a large meal; it helps to keep your metabolism going and stops you feeling hungry (and in danger of nibbling) or bored.

SUGGESTED DAY'S PLAN

BREAKFAST

½ grapefruit or 1 small glass orange juice.

1 boiled or poached egg; *or* 25 g/1 oz cereal with skimmed milk from allowance.

Toast with a scraping of butter, margarine or low-calorie spread.

Coffee or tea with skimmed milk.

LUNCH

840 kJ/200 calorie fish or meat, or 50 g/2 oz cheese with a vegetarian dish.

Salad or green vegetable. Potato or pasta if desired.

420 kJ/100 calorie pudding or fruit.

Coffee with skimmed milk from allowance.

TEA TIME

Tea with lemon or skimmed milk from allowance and second slice of bread with a scraping of butter if wanted and if you haven't had a potato or pasta for lunch or plan to do so for dinner.

DINNER

Either:

420 kJ/100 calorie soup or starter.
840 kJ/200 calorie meat or fish dish.
420 kJ/100 calorie pudding.

Or:

420 kJ/100 calorie soup, starter *or* pudding.

1250 kJ/300 calorie meat or fish dish.

Salad, green vegetable or about 50 g/2 oz helping root vegetable (swede, turnip, parsnip).

Lunch and dinner are interchangeable, depending on when you like the larger meal.

If 5000 kJ/1200 calories count does not take off the weight at around 1 kg/2 lb a week then reduce the day's intake, by eating lower caloried dishes generally (or cutting out starters and puddings), to 4200 kJ/1000 calories but on no account reduce any further unless you have your doctor's permission.

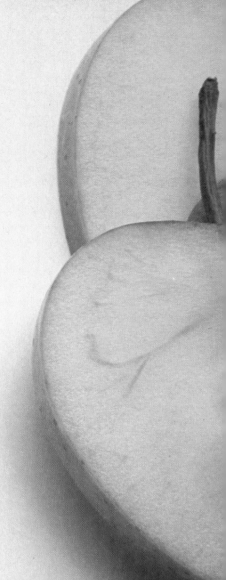

COOKING METHODS

You may find some of the cooking methods in this book a little unusual at first, but they are very straightforward once you have got used to them. Except for a blender and non-stick frying pan or saucepan you need no special equipment.

CASSEROLES

Most of the casserole recipes suggest you put the meat straight into the casserole; but if you like you may seal the meat very quickly on both sides first either in a non-stick pan with no fat (or a low-calorie fat or spray oil, adding 60 kJ/15 calories per dessertspoon) or lightly grill before putting the meat into the casserole.

MEAT

Meat must have all visible fat removed. Poultry must have all skin removed otherwise the kJ/calorie count will be higher.

YOGURT

The yogurt used is plain, low-fat unsweetened yogurt bought commercially. You may use home-made provided it is made with skimmed milk with no fat added. Do not let yogurt boil as it will curdle.

CURD CHEESE

The curd cheese used is commercial low fat curd cheese, except in the cheese-cake recipe which uses a skimmed milk curd cheese, available in supermarkets.

ENTERTAINING

Just because you are dieting to lose weight, this does not mean that you have to stop entertaining or being entertained. Just eat your daily food allowance only. There follows some suggested menus for entertaining.

LUNCH PARTY OR SUNDAY LUNCH

Salmon Pâté (page 29)

Lamb Stuffed with Apricots (page 86)
Courgettes Lyonnaise (page 109)
Baked potatoes (*for guests only if you have stuffing*)

Bean, Tomato and Pepper Salad (page 44)

Coffee Sorbet (page 121)

About 1920 kJ/460 calories

Serve with claret or burgundy, whipped cream and brown sugar *all for guests only.*

SUPPER PARTY FOR TWELVE

Stuffed Breast of Veal (*you will have to prepare 2 for 12 people*) (page 97)

Mushroom, Courgette & Tomato Salad (page 51)

Green Salad (page 44)

Triple Vegetable Ring (page 24)

Rosy Pears (page 118)

Pavlova (page 116)

Cheese & Biscuits (*for guests only*)

About 1670 kJ/400 calories

Serve with Italian white wine, cream and sugar *all for guests only.*

Opposite: a selection of dishes from the suggested Lunch Party or Sunday Lunch menu.

HEIGHT & WEIGHT CHARTS (weigh without clothes on)

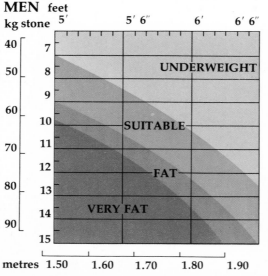

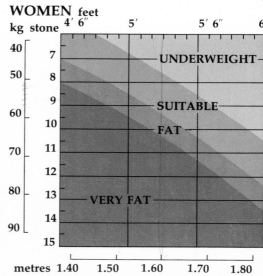

FOOD AND DRINK VALUE TABLE (in most cases, figures have been rounded up or down for ease of calculation)

Food and drink	KJ/calorie per 25 g/1 oz or 25 ml/1 fl oz	KJ/calorie per 100 g/4 oz or 120 ml/4 fl oz
ALCOHOLIC DRINKS		
Beer		
bitter	40/10	170/40
mild	20/5	80/20
Campari	290/70	1170/280
Cider		
dry or sweet	40/10	170/40
vintage	125/30	500/120
Cognac	270/65	1090/260
Dubonnet	190/45	750/180
Gin	270/65	1090/260
Grand Marnier	380/90	1500/360
Keg Bitter	40/10	170/40
Lager – bottled	40/10	170/40
Port	190/45	750/180
Rum	270/65	1090/260
Sherry		
dry	145/35	585/140
medium	145/35	585/140
sweet	170/40	670/160
Vermouth		
dry	145/35	585/140
sweet	190/45	750/180
Vodka	270/65	1090/260
Whisky	270/65	1090/260
Wine		
red	80/20	330/80
rosé	80/20	330/80
white	80/20	330/80
sweet	100/25	420/100
FOODS		
Anchovies	190/45	750/180
Apples		
raw	40/10	170/40
dried	270/65	1090/260
juice	40/10	170/40
Apricots		
raw	20/5	80/20
dried	210/50	840/200
canned	125/30	500/120
Artichokes		
globe	20/5	80/20
Jerusalem	20/5	80/20
Asparagus		
fresh	20/5	80/20
canned	12/3	50/12
Aubergine – raw	20/5	80/20
Avocado	270/65	1090/260
Bacon – lean, no fat	270/65	1090/260
Bamboo shoots	40/10	170/40

Food and drink	KJ/calorie per 25 g/1 oz or 25 ml/1 fl oz	KJ/calorie per 100 g/4 oz or 120 ml/4 fl oz
Bass	100/25	420/100
Beans – raw		
French	8/2	35/8
runner	20/5	80/20
broad	60/15	250/60
butter	100/25	420/100
chick peas	100/25	420/100
haricot	100/25	420/100
red kidney	100/25	420/100
Bean sprouts	16/4	65/16
Beef		
lean, no fat	250/60	1000/240
steak	230/55	920/220
minced	250/60	1000/240
stewing	250/60	1000/240
Beetroot – raw	40/10	170/40
Blackberries – raw	40/10	170/40
Blackcurrants – raw	40/10	170/40
Bread		
bap	380/90	
brown	270/65	
currant	290/70	
granary	250/60	
Hovis	270/65	
malt	290/70	
croissant	440/105	1090/260 (1 croissant)
crumpet	310/75	
wholemeal	250/60	1000/240
Breakfast cereals	380–440 /90–105	1500–1760 /360–420
Bream – raw	100/25	420/100
Broad beans	60/15	250/60
Brussels sprouts – boiled	20/5	80/20
Butter	880/210	3510/840
Buttermilk	40/10	170/40
Cabbage		
raw	20/5	80/20
red	20/5	80/20
Carrots		
raw	20/5	80/20
canned	20/5	80/20
Cauliflower – raw	20/5	80/20
Celery – raw	8/2	35/8
Cheese		
Austrian smoked	310/75	1250/300
Bel Paese	330/80	1340/320
Caerphilly	420/100	1670/400
Camembert	355/85	1420/340
Cheddar	420–500 /100–120	1670–2000 /400–480
Cheshire	460/110	1840/440
cottage	125/30	500/120
curd	170/40	670/160
Danish Blue	420/100	1670/400

FOOD AND DRINK VALUE TABLE (in most cases, figures have been rounded up or down for ease of calculation)

Food and drink	KJ/calorie per 25 g/1 oz or 25 ml/1 fl oz	KJ/calorie per 100 g/4 oz or 120 ml/4 fl oz
Dolcelatte	400/95	1590/380
Double Gloucester	420/100	1670/400
Edam	355/85	1420/340
Emmenthal	460/110	1840/440
full fat soft	520/125	2090/500
Gouda	355/85	1420/340
Gruyère	500/120	2000/480
Lancashire	420/100	1670/400
Leicester	460/110	1840/440
Mozzarella	400/95	1590/380
Parmesan	500/120	2000/480
Port Salut	380/90	1500/360
processed	380/90	1500/360
Ricotta	290/70	1170/280
Roquefort	420/100	1670/400
Sage Derby	460/110	1840/440
St Paulin	380/90	1500/360
Stilton	540/130	2170/520
Wensleydale	460/110	1840/440
Cherries		
raw	40/10	170/40
glacé	250/60	1000/240
Chicken		
meat only, no skin	125/30	500/120
poussin	80/20	330/80
Chicory – raw	12/3	50/12
Chocolate		
milk	630/150	2500/600
plain	630/150	2500/600
drinking	440/105	1760/420
Cod – raw	80/20	330/80
Cod roe – smoked	125/30	500/120
Cornflour	420/100	1670/400
Courgettes – raw	12/3	50/12
Crab – boiled	145/35	585/140
Crayfish – shelled	125/30	500/120
Cream		
clotted	670/160	2680/640
single	250/60	1000/240
double	520/125	2090/500
soured	230/55	920/220
Crispbread	380–420 /90–100	1500–1670 /360–400
Cucumber		
raw	12/3	50/12
pickled	12/3	50/12
Curry powder	270/65	1090/260
Custard powder	420/100	1670/400
Damsons – raw	40/10	170/40
Dates – dried	250/60	1000/240
Digestive biscuit	210/50 (each biscuit)	840/200 (4 biscuits)
Dried, skimmed milk	420/100	1670/400
Duck – meat only, no skin	250/60	1170/280

Food and drink	KJ/calorie per 25 g/1 oz or 25 ml/1 fl oz	KJ/calorie per 100 g/4 oz or 120 ml/4 fl oz
Eel – raw	210/50	840/200
Egg (depending on size)	each 170–250/40–60	
Endive	12/3	50/12
Figs		
green raw	40/10	170/40
dried	250/60	1000/240
Fish		
anchovy (no oil)	190/45	750/180
bass	100/25	420/100
bream	100/25	420/100
cod	100/25	420/100
cod roe, smoked	125/30	500/120
crab	145/35	585/140
crayfish, shelled	125/30	500/120
haddock, raw	80/20	330/80
" , smoked	80/20	330/80
hake	100/25	420/100
halibut	125/30	500/120
kipper	250/60	1000/240
lobster	145/35	585/140
mackerel, raw	250/60	1000/240
" , smoked	380/90	1090/360
pilchard (no oil)	230/55	920/220
plaice	100/25	420/100
prawns, shelled	125/30	500/120
salmon	210/50	840/200
scallop, raw	125/30	500/120
scampi, boiled	125/30	500/120
skate, raw	80/20	330/80
sole, raw	80/20	330/80
trout, raw	125/30	500/120
tuna (no oil)	290/70	1170/280
turbot, raw	100/25	420/100
whiting, raw	100/25	420/100
Flour		
plain	420/100	1670/400
wholemeal	400/95	1590/380
Fruit and Fruit juices		
apples	40/10	250/60 (average size)
apple juice	40/10	170/40
apricot, fresh	20/5	80/20 (average size)
" , dried	210/50	840/200
" , canned	125/30	500/120
avocado	270/65	1045/250 (½ average)
banana	60/15	420/100 (average size)
blackberry	40/10	170/40
blackcurrant	40/10	170/40
cherries, raw	40/10	170/40
" , canned	80/20	330/80
clementine	40/10	210/50 (average size)
cranberries, raw	16/4	65/16
damsons	40/10	170/40

FOOD AND DRINK VALUE TABLE — (in most cases, figures have been rounded up or down for ease of calculation)

Food and drink	KJ/calorie per 25 g/1 oz or 25 ml/1 fl oz	KJ/calorie per 100 g/4 oz or 120 ml/4 fl oz
figs, raw	40/10	210/50 (average size)
'' , dried	460/110	1840/440
gooseberries	20–40/5–10	80–170/20–40
grapes, raw	80/20	330/80
'' , juice	80/20	330/80
grapefruit, fresh	12/3	50/12 (½ portion)
'' , unsweetened juice	40/10	170/40
greengage, raw	60/15	250/60
lemon, raw		20/5 (average size)
'' , juice	8/2	35/8
loganberries	20/5	80/20
lychees, raw	80/20	330/80
'' , canned	80/20	330/80
mandarin, raw	40/10	170/40 (average size)
melon	20/5	
mulberries, raw	40/10	170/40
'' , canned	100/25	420/100
nectarines, raw	60/15	250/60 (average size)
oranges	40/10	210/50 (average size)
'' , unsweetened juice	40/10	170/40
passion fruit, raw	40/10	
peaches, fresh	40/10	210/50 (average size)
'' , canned	100/25	420/100
pears, fresh	40/10	250/60 (average size)
'' , canned	80/20	330/80
pineapple, fresh	60/15	250/60
'' , canned	80/20	330/80
'' , unsweetened juice	60/15	250/60
plums, raw	40/10	170/40
prunes, dried	170/40	670/160
'' , unsweetened juice	80/20	330/80
raisins	290/70	1170/280
raspberries, raw	20/5	80/20
redcurrants, raw	20/5	80/20
rhubarb, raw	8/2	35/8
satsuma	20/5	60/15 (average size)
strawberries, raw	40/10	170/40
'' , canned	100/25	420/100
tangerine, fresh	20/5	60/15 (average size)
Gelatine	400/95	1590/380
Goose – no skin	250/60	1000/240
Gooseberries	20–40/5–10	80–170/20–40
Grapes	80/20	330/80
Grapefruit – fresh	12/3	50/12 (½ portion)
Gravy browning	330/80	1340/320
Grouse – roast	210/50	
Haddock		
fresh	80/20	330/80
smoked	80/20	330/80
Hake	80/20	330/80
Halibut	100/25	420/100
Honey	330/80	
Horseradish		
raw	60/15	250/60
cream sauce	250/60	
Ice cream	190/45	750/180
Jam	310/75	1250/300
Jelly – made with cubes	80/20	330/80
Kipper	330/80	1340/320
Lamb – lean, raw	210–290 /50–70	840–1170 /200–280
Leeks	20/5	80/20
Lentils – boiled	125/30	500/120
Lettuce	12/3	50/12
Lime juice – bottled	125/30	500/120
Low fat spread	420/100	1670/400
Macaroni – raw	420/100	1670/400
Mackerel		
fresh	270/65	1000/240
smoked	380/90	1500/360
Margarine	920/220	3680/880
Marrow	12/3	50/12
Matzo biscuit	460/110	1840/440
Meat – all visible fat removed, no fat used in cooking		
bacon/gammon, raw	270/65	1090/260
'' , grilled rashers, without fat	270/65	1090/260
'' , grilled rashers, with fat	500–585 /120–140	2000–2340 /480–560
beef—raw, good quality	250/60	1000/240
'' , minced	270/65	1090/260
'' , corned	250/60	1000/240
'' , silverside	290/70	1170/280
'' , stewing steak, no fat	225/50	840/200
ham boiled, no fat, Prosciutto	290/70	1170/280
'' , or Parma	270/65	1090/260
lamb lean, raw	210/290 /50–70	840/1170 /200–280
'' , breast	460/110	1840/440
Mortadella	355/85	1420/340
pork, lean, raw	210/50	840/200
salami, lean	355/85	1420/340
sausages, beef, grilled	230/55	920/220
'' , pork, grilled	380/90	1500/360
veal, lean, no fat	125/30	500/120
Melon	20/5	80/20

FOOD AND DRINK VALUE TABLE (in most cases, figures have been rounded up or down for ease of calculation)

Food and drink	KJ/calorie per 25 g/1 oz or 25 ml/1 fl oz	KJ/calorie per 100 g/4 oz or 120 ml/4 fl oz
Milk, cow's		
one pint	80/20	330/80
sterilized	80/20	330/80
long life	80/20	330/80
skimmed liquid	40/10	170/40
powdered skimmed	420/100	1670/400
Mint sauce – in jars	125/30	500/120
Mushrooms	8/2	35/8
Nuts		
almonds	670/160	2680/640
brazils	730/175	2930/700
cashews	650/155	2590/620
hazelnuts	460/110	1840/440
peanuts	670/160	2680/640
walnuts	630/150	2500/600
Oatmeal – raw	480/115	1920/460
Offal		
brain, boiled	170/40	670/160
heart, raw	145/35	585/140
kidney, raw	100/25	420/100
liver, raw	190/45	750/180
sweetbread, raw	170/40	670/160
tongue	230/55	920/220
Olives	100/25	420/100
Olive oil	1045/250	4200/1000
Onions	20/5	80/20
Orange marmalade	310/75	1250/300
Oranges	40/10	170/40
Parsnips	60/15	250/60
Pastry		
cooked choux	400/95	1590/380
cooked flaky	670/160	2680/640
cooked short	630/150	2500/600
Pâté, bought	400/95	1590/380
Peaches – fresh	40/10	170/40
Peanut butter	730/175	2930/700
Pearl barley – raw	420/100	1670/400
Pears – fresh	60/15	250/60
Peas	80/20	330/80
Pheasant	250/60	1000/240
Pineapple – fresh	60/15	250/60
Pigeon	270/65	1090/260
Plaice	100/25	420/100
Plums	40/10	170/40
Pork, lean raw	210/50	840/200
Potatoes		
boiled	100/25	420/100
mashed	145/35	585/140
baked	125/30	500/120
roast	190/45	750/180
chips	290/70	1170/280

Food and drink	KJ/calorie per 25 g/1 oz or 25 ml/1 fl oz	KJ/calorie per 100 g/4 oz or 120 ml/4 fl oz
Quiche Lorraine	460/110	1840/440
Rabbit – raw	145/35	585/140
Radishes	20/5	80/20
Raisins	290/70	1170/280
Raspberries	20/5	80/20
Rice – raw	440/105	1760/420
Salmon	210/50	840/200
Salsify – raw	20/5	80/20
Sardines – drained	250/60	1000/240
Sauerkraut – canned	20/5	80/20
Shortbread	610/145	2420/580
Skate	80/20	330/80
Sole	80/20	330/80
Soya beans	480/115	1920/460
Spinach	20/5	80/20
Spring greens	12/3	40/10
Spring onions	20/5	80/20
Starch-reduced crispbread	460/110	1840/440
Starch-reduced rolls	460/110	1840/440
Strawberries	40/10	170/40
Sugar	460/110	1840/440
Sultanas	290/70	1170/280
Sweetcorn – canned	80/20	330/80
Tagliatelle	440/105	1760/420
Tangerine – fresh	20/5	80/20
Tapioca	420/100	1670/400
Taramasalata	380/90	1500/360
Tomatoes – raw	20/5	80/20
Tuna – no oil	290/70	1170/280
Turbot – raw	100/25	420/100
Turkey – no skin	125/30	500/120
Turnips	20/5	80/20
Turnip tops	20/5	80/20
Vegetable oils	1045/250	4200/1000
Venison – raw	170/40	670/160
Wheatgerm	420/100	1670/400
Whiting – raw	100/25	420/100
Winkles	20/5	60/15
Woodcock – roast	80/20	330/80
Yeast		
fresh	60/15	250/60
dried	210/50	840/200
Yeast extract	210/50	840/200

SOUPS & STARTERS

CHICKEN STOCK

Preparation time: 5 minutes, plus chilling
Cooking time: 2 hours
KJ/calorie count: 355/85 per recipe

1 chicken carcass
1 litre/1¾ pints water
4 sticks celery with leaves, trimmed and chopped
1 large onion, peeled and chopped
1 bay leaf
salt
freshly ground black pepper

Stock is the most important part of a soup – the better the stock, the better the soup. Even if you have to rely on stock cubes, try to blend them with water in which you have boiled vegetables as it will taste much richer.

1. Put all the ingredients in a saucepan and bring to the boil. Skim off any scum with a spoon.
2. Cover and simmer for 2 hours.
3. Strain the stock and refrigerate for about 3 hours.
4. When set remove all fat from the top.

VARIATION:
Beef stock: Use the same method but substitute beef bones for the chicken carcass, covering them with water.

FISH STOCK

Preparation time: 5 minutes
Cooking time: 30 minutes
KJ/calorie count: 285/68 per recipe

450 g/1 lb white fish bones e.g. sole, plaice, coley, heads and pieces
600 ml/1 pint water
1 large onion, peeled and chopped
2 sticks celery, trimmed and chopped
2 carrots, peeled and chopped
1 bay leaf
salt
freshly ground black pepper

1. Rinse the fish thoroughly. Put all ingredients in a saucepan and bring to the boil. Remove any scum with a spoon.
2. Cover and simmer for 30 minutes.
3. Strain and refrigerate until needed.

Top left: Fish stock
Top right: Chicken stock
Bottom: Spinach soup

SPINACH SOUP

Preparation time: 5 minutes
Cooking time: 20 minutes
KJ/calorie count: 80/20

350 g/12 oz spinach, washed
900 ml/1¾ pints chicken stock
2 tablespoons lemon juice
salt
freshly ground black pepper

1. Put the spinach, stock, lemon juice, salt and pepper into a saucepan and bring to the boil. Cover and simmer for about 15 minutes until the spinach is thoroughly cooked.
2. Allow to cool slightly then pour into a blender and liquidize until smooth. Alternatively, rub through a sieve.
3. Return the soup to the pan and reheat.

WATERCRESS SOUP

Preparation time: 10 minutes
Cooking time: 20 minutes
KJ/calorie count: 290/70

4 bunches watercress, washed
900 ml/1½ pints chicken stock or
   900 ml/1½ pints water and 3
   chicken stock cubes
25 g/1 oz chopped onion
50 g/2 oz dried skimmed milk
   powder
salt
freshly ground black pepper

1. Remove any discoloured parts from the watercress. Reserve 4 sprigs for garnish.
2. Chop the watercress stalks, then place all the watercress in a saucepan with the stock and chopped onion. Bring to the boil, cover and simmer for 15 minutes.
3. Allow to cool slightly, then pour into a blender and liquidize until smooth. Alternatively, rub through a sieve.
4. Return the soup to the pan and reheat.
5. Remove from the heat and stir in the skimmed milk powder slowly (if the mixture is too hot it will go lumpy). Add the salt and pepper to taste and serve garnished with the watercress sprigs.

VARIATION:
Instead of watercress use a medium lettuce, well shredded.

CUCUMBER SOUP

Preparation time: 5 minutes
Cooking time: 15 minutes
KJ/calorie count: 230/55

1 large cucumber, peeled and
   chopped
900 ml/1½ pints chicken stock
1 teaspoon Worcestershire sauce
salt
freshly ground black pepper
4 teaspoons dried skimmed milk
   powder

1. Steam the cucumber pieces for about 10 minutes.
2. Put the cucumber in a blender with the stock, Worcestershire sauce and salt and pepper. Liquidize until smooth.
3. Pour into a saucepan and reheat until almost boiling. When serving, stir 1 teaspoon skimmed milk powder into each bowl of soup.

VEGETABLE SOUP

Preparation time: 15 minutes
Cooking time: 25 minutes
KJ/calorie count: 330/80

275 g/10 oz carrots, scraped and
   chopped
275 g/10 oz swede, trimmed and
   chopped
3 celery sticks, trimmed and
   chopped
2 onions, peeled and chopped
salt
freshly ground black pepper
900 ml/1½ pints stock
1 teaspoon chopped fresh
   tarragon or ½ teaspoon dried
   tarragon (optional)
8 teaspoons dried skimmed milk
   powder

1. Place all the vegetables in a saucepan, add salt and pepper and pour in the stock.
2. Bring to the boil and skim off the scum with a spoon. Cover and simmer for about 20 minutes until the vegetables are soft. Add the tarragon.
3. Allow to cool slightly then pour into a blender and liquidize until smooth. Alternatively, rub through a sieve.
4. Return the soup to the pan and reheat.
5. When serving, stir 2 teaspoons skimmed milk powder into each bowl. Non-slimmers can add a spoonful of single cream to each bowl.

Top left: Pea and curd soup
Top centre: Watercress soup
Top right: Curried parsnip soup
Bottom left: Vegetable soup
Bottom right: Cucumber soup

CURRIED PARSNIP SOUP

Preparation time: 5 minutes
Cooking time: 25 minutes
KJ/calorie count: 420/100

450 g/1 lb parsnips, scraped or
    peeled and chopped
900 ml/1½ pints chicken stock
pinch of salt
freshly ground black pepper
1 teaspoon curry powder, or to
    taste

1. Place the chopped parsnip in a
saucepan with the stock, salt and pepper.
Bring to the boil, cover and simmer for
about 20 minutes until the parsnips are
tender.
2. Allow to cool slightly then pour into a
blender and liquidize until smooth, adding
the curry powder. Alternatively, rub
through a sieve.
3. Return the soup to the pan and reheat.

PEA & CURD SOUP

Preparation time: 5 minutes
Cooking time: 8 minutes
KJ/calorie count: 500/120

225 g/8 oz shelled peas
300 ml/½ pint chicken stock or
    300 ml/½ pint water and 2
    chicken stock cubes
225 g/8 oz curd cheese
salt
freshly ground black pepper
1 tablespoon chopped fresh mint
    (optional)

1. Put the peas in a saucepan and add the
stock. Bring to the boil, cover and simmer
for about 5 minutes until the peas are
tender.
2. Allow to cool slightly then pour into a
blender. Add the curd cheese and
crumbled stock cubes, if used, and
liquidize until smooth.
3. Return the soup to the pan, taste and
adjust the seasoning, then bring to the boil
and simmer for 1 minute.
4. Pour into soup bowls and garnish each
bowl with chopped mint.

VARIATION:
Instead of peas use 450 g/1 lb carrots,
scraped and thinly sliced.
KJ/calorie count: 420/100

BEETROOT SOUP

Preparation time: 15 minutes
Cooking time: about 35 minutes
KJ/calorie count: 210/50

3 medium beetroots, scrubbed or peeled, grated
900 ml/1½ pints chicken or beef stock
25 g/1 oz chopped onion
salt
freshly ground black pepper
4 dessertspoons plain unsweetened yogurt

1. Place the grated beetroot in a saucepan with the stock, onion, and salt and pepper. Bring to the boil.
2. Skim if necessary and simmer for about 30 minutes until the beetroot is very soft.
3. Allow to cool slightly and pour into a blender. Liquidize until smooth. Alternatively, rub through a sieve.
4. Return the soup to the rinsed out pan and reheat thoroughly.
5. Serve in individual bowls with a spoonful of yogurt.

VARIATIONS:
Add a spoonful of grated horseradish to each bowl of soup.
KJ/calorie count: 150/36 per 25 g/1 oz
For a **Cherry and Beetroot Soup**, cook 225 g/8 oz stoned morello or black cherries in enough water to cover, adding artificial sweetener to taste. Add to the beetroot soup after liquidizing. Serve hot or cold.
KJ/calorie count: 355/85

MIXED VEGETABLE & NOODLE SOUP

Preparation time: 15 minutes
Cooking time: 25 minutes
KJ/calorie count: 585/140

450 g/1 lb mixed vegetables, peeled and diced, e.g. carrots, onions, courgettes, celery
100 g/4 oz cabbage, shredded
600 ml/1 pint stock
300 ml/½ pint tomato juice
100 g/4 oz noodles or small pasta
salt
freshly ground black pepper
½-1 garlic clove, peeled and crushed

1. Place all the vegetables in a saucepan with the stock and tomato juice.
2. Bring to the boil, add the pasta, skim, cover and simmer for about 20 minutes, adding salt, pepper and garlic during cooking.

CHILLED APPLE SOUP

Preparation time: 15 minutes, plus chilling
Cooking time: 25 minutes
KJ/calorie count: 270/65

450 g/1 lb cooking apples, peeled, cored and sliced
1 tablespoon lemon juice
artificial liquid sweetener, to taste
1 teaspoon ground cinnamon or mixed spice
900 ml/1½ pints chicken stock
1 teaspoon cornflour
lemon slices, to garnish

1. Place the apples, lemon juice, artificial sweetener, spice and stock in a saucepan and bring to the boil. Skim, then cover and simmer for about 20 minutes until the apples are soft.
2. Allow to cool slightly and pour into a blender. Liquidize until smooth. Alternatively, rub through a sieve.
3. Mix the cornflour with a little water and add to the soup. Return to the rinsed out saucepan and stir over the heat until it thickens.
4. Chill thoroughly and serve garnished with lemon slices.

Top left: Beetroot soup
Top right: Dubarry soup
Bottom left: Mixed vegetable and noodle soup
Bottom right: Chilled apple soup

DUBARRY SOUP

Preparation time: 15 minutes
Cooking time: 25 minutes
KJ/calorie count: 420/100

1 medium cauliflower, trimmed
2 medium potatoes, peeled and
   thinly sliced
900 ml/1½ pints chicken stock
2 dessertspoons dried skimmed
   milk powder
pinch of grated nutmeg
salt
freshly ground black pepper

1. Cut the cauliflower into small florets.
2. Place the cauliflower, potatoes and stock in a saucepan and bring to the boil. Skim, then cover and simmer for about 20 minutes until the vegetables are soft.
3. Allow to cool slightly and pour into a blender. Add the skimmed milk powder, nutmeg and salt and pepper to taste. Liquidize until a smooth thin cream. Alternatively, rub through a sieve.
4. Return the soup to the rinsed out pan and reheat thoroughly.

5. If liked, garnish with a pinch of grated nutmeg.

VARIATION:
For a more substantial soup, add grated Cheddar cheese to taste.

MUSSEL CHOWDER

Preparation time: 5 minutes
Cooking time: 30 minutes
KJ/calorie count: 840/200

1 green pepper, cored, seeded and chopped
50 g/2 oz chopped onion
350 g/12 oz potatoes, peeled and chopped
1 litre/1¾ pints chicken or fish stock
450 g/1 lb shelled mussels, cooked or canned
salt
freshly ground black pepper
4 tablespoons dried skimmed milk powder

If you are cooking fresh mussels, you will need to buy about 1·5 kg/3 lb mussels in their shells. Scrub them, pulling off the beards and discarding any that are open. Cook quickly in about 200 ml/⅓ pint stock for 5-6 minutes. Drain, then discard any shells that have not opened.

1. Put the pepper, onion, potatoes and stock in a saucepan and bring to the boil. Skim off any scum with a spoon, cover and simmer for 20 minutes.
2. Add the mussels and salt and pepper, then simmer for a further 5 minutes.
3. When serving, stir in a tablespoon of skimmed milk powder to each bowl. Non-slimmers can stir a tablespoon of single cream into each bowl.

CONSOMMÉ

Preparation time: 15 minutes
Cooking time: 1 hour
KJ/calorie count: 210/50

75 g/3 oz carrots, peeled and thinly sliced
75 g/3 oz celery, trimmed and thinly sliced
4 tomatoes, skinned
1 green pepper, cored, seeded and sliced
1 litre/1¾ pints beef stock
1 bay leaf
1 teaspoon chopped fresh parsley
25 g/1 oz chopped onion
salt
freshly ground black pepper
2 egg whites, beaten to soft peaks
4 tablespoons sherry

1. Put all the vegetables into a saucepan with the stock, herbs, onion and salt and pepper to taste.
2. Add the beaten egg whites slowly, stirring.
3. Bring to the boil, then simmer gently for 1 hour.
4. Strain through a cheesecloth into a tureen and stir in the sherry.

Above front: Iced summer soup
Above back: Gazpacho

LEMON SOUP

Preparation time: 10 minutes
Cooking time: 10 minutes
KJ/calorie count: 170/40

900 ml/1½ pints chicken stock or 900 ml/1½ pints boiling water and 2 chicken stock cubes
1 egg
6 tablespoons lemon juice
½ teaspoon Worcestershire sauce (optional)

This soup is also good served cold.

1. Pour the stock into a saucepan and bring to the boil or dissolve the stock cubes in the boiling water.
2. Beat the egg with the lemon juice in a bowl and add the Worcestershire sauce, if used.
3. If necessary remove the stock from the heat and leave to stand for a couple of minutes. Slowly beat in the egg and lemon mixture.
4. Return to a very low heat until the mixture thickens slightly, stirring. Do not let the soup boil as the egg will curdle.

GAZPACHO

Preparation time: 20 minutes
KJ/calorie count: 500/120

1 large cucumber
175 g/6 oz green pepper
175 g/6 oz red pepper
3 garlic cloves, peeled
2 tablespoons olive oil
2 tablespoons wine vinegar
900 ml/1½ pints tomato juice, chilled
salt
freshly ground black pepper

1. Cut half the cucumber, green and red pepper into small pieces and arrange in serving dishes for garnishing.
2. Grate the remaining cucumber and finely chop the remaining peppers.
3. Put in a blender with the garlic, olive oil and wine vinegar. Liquidize until smooth.
4. Stir this mixture into the chilled tomato juice and add salt and pepper to taste.
5. Serve in a large tureen with cubes of ice floating in it, and the dishes of garnishes around.

ICED SUMMER SOUP

Preparation time: 8 minutes, plus chilling
KJ/calorie count: 585/140

1 large cucumber, peeled and sliced
225 g/8 oz courgettes, cooked and chopped
225 g/8 oz curd cheese
600 ml/1 pint chicken stock
pinch of curry powder

1. Put all the ingredients into a blender. Liquidize for 3 minutes until well mixed (switch the machine on and off several times).
2. Turn the mixture into a large jug and place in the refrigerator for 2-3 hours until completely chilled. (To chill the soup quickly, add ice cubes to the blender.)
3. To serve, pour into individual soup bowls. Non-slimmers can add a tablespoon of cream to each bowl.

Below left: Mussel chowder
Centre: Consommé
Below right: Lemon soup

TRIPLE VEGETABLE RING

Preparation time: about 30 minutes, plus setting

Cooking time: spinach – 10 minutes, carrots – 20 minutes

KJ/calorie count: 5430/1300 whole dish; about 420/100 per serving

SPINACH RING:

15 g/½ oz powdered gelatine
450 g/1 lb cooked spinach
1 tablespoon lemon juice
225 g/8 oz curd cheese
salt
freshly ground black pepper

CARROT RING:

450 g/1 lb carrots, peeled and thinly sliced
120 ml/4 fl oz unsweetened orange juice
pinch of grated nutmeg
salt
freshly ground black pepper
15 g/½ oz powdered gelatine
225 g/8 oz curd cheese

CUCUMBER RING:

15 g/½ oz powdered gelatine
1½ cucumbers, peeled and diced
1 chicken stock cube, crumbled
pinch of ground mace
225 g/8 oz curd cheese

This is an excellent dish to serve when entertaining almost any number up to 15 people. Make the ring in a clear glass dish about 23 cm/9 inches wide and 13 cm/5 inches deep; it will look as pretty as it is delicious! Each ring takes about 3 hours to set so start making it the previous day.

1. For the spinach ring, put the gelatine in a teacup of water, stand the cup in a bowl of hot water and stir until dissolved.
2. Place the spinach, lemon juice, curd cheese and dissolved gelatine in a blender and liquidize until smooth. Taste and adjust the seasoning.
3. Pour into the glass dish and leave to set.
4. For the carrot ring, place the carrots, orange juice, nutmeg, salt and pepper in a saucepan and bring to the boil. Simmer for about 20 minutes until the carrots are soft.
5. Put the carrots in a liquidizer with enough cooking liquid to blend the carrots.
6. Put the gelatine in a teacup of water, stand the cup in a bowl of hot water and stir until dissolved.
7. Add the curd cheese and dissolved gelatine to the carrot purée and blend until smooth.
8. Pour on top of the set spinach ring and leave to set.
9. For the cucumber ring, put the gelatine in a teacup of water, stand the cup in a bowl of hot water and stir until dissolved.
10. Place the cucumber, stock cube, mace and curd cheese in a blender and liquidize until smooth.
11. Add the dissolved gelatine and liquidize again until smooth. This mixture will be a little more runny than the other two.
12. Pour on top of the set carrot ring and leave to set.

PRAWNS IN ASPIC

Preparation time: 10 minutes, plus setting

Cooking time: 5 minutes

KJ/calorie count: 500/120

15 g/½ oz sachet of aspic
350 g/12 oz peeled prawns
1 × 225 g/8 oz can asparagus tips, drained
100 g/4 oz cooked peas
lemon slices, to garnish

1. Make up the aspic according to the directions on the packet and pour into a straight-sided bowl.
2. Add the prawns, asparagus tips and peas in layers and leave to set.
3. Turn out and garnish with lemon slices. Alternatively, make in individual dishes and leave unmoulded.

Top left: Triple vegetable ring
Bottom left: Prawns in aspic
Top right: Athenian vegetables
Centre: Spiced artichokes
Bottom right: Turkish aubergines

ATHENIAN VEGETABLES

Preparation time: 20 minutes, plus
cooling and marinating
Cooking time: 15-20 minutes
KJ/calorie count: 80/20, plus dressing

---

100 g/4 oz cauliflower florets,
trimmed
100 g/4 oz broccoli, trimmed
100 g/4 oz carrots, peeled and cut
into sticks
100 g/4 oz green beans, trimmed
and cut into pieces
120 ml/4 fl oz lemon juice
1 teaspoon ground coriander
1 teaspoon dried rosemary
salt
freshly ground black pepper
Lemon Vinaigrette (page 57)

1. Place the vegetables in a saucepan and cover with water. Add the lemon juice, coriander, rosemary, salt and pepper.
2. Bring to the boil, cover and simmer for 10-15 minutes until just cooked but still firm. Allow the vegetables to cool in the cooking liquid.
3. Drain the vegetables and arrange them in separate piles on 4 plates.
4. Pour the Lemon Vinaigrette over and leave to marinate for 2-3 hours before serving.

SPICED ARTICHOKES

Preparation time: 15 minutes, plus
marinating
Cooking time: 15 minutes
KJ/calorie count: 170/40, plus
dressing

---

900 g/2 lb Jerusalem artichokes,
peeled
salt
1 dessertspoon vinegar

DRESSING:
Lemon Vinaigrette (page 57)
1 garlic clove, peeled and crushed
pinch of grated nutmeg
pinch of ground mace

1. Place the artichokes in a saucepan of boiling salted water with the vinegar added. Cover and simmer for about 15 minutes until tender. Drain and leave to cool.
2. Slice the artichokes and transfer to a serving dish.
3. Add the garlic and spices to the vinaigrette dressing and pour over the artichokes.
4. Leave to marinate for about 3 hours. Serve chilled.

TURKISH AUBERGINES

Preparation time: 15 minutes
Cooking time: about 20 minutes
KJ/calorie count: 380/90

---

4 medium aubergines
salt
1 teaspoon ground mace
olive oil

DRESSING:
300 ml/½ pint plain unsweetened
yogurt
1 dessertspoon olive oil
1 dessertspoon lemon or orange
juice
pinch of ground mace
salt
freshly ground black pepper
shredded orange rind, to garnish

1. Halve the aubergines lengthways, sprinkle with salt and mace.
2. Lightly oil pieces of foil large enough to completely enclose each aubergine. Wrap the aubergines and bake in a preheated oven at 200°C, 400°F, Gas Mark 6 for about 20 minutes until soft.
3. Meanwhile, mix the yogurt, olive oil, lemon or orange juice, mace and salt and pepper together.
4. Unwrap the aubergines, pour the cold sauce over the hot aubergine halves and garnish with shredded orange rind.

JELLIED GRAPEFRUIT & CUCUMBER SOUP

Preparation time: 10 minutes, plus setting
Cooking time: 10 minutes
KJ/calorie count: 420/100

1 litre/1¾ pints unsweetened grapefruit juice
25 g/1 oz powdered gelatine
salt
freshly ground black pepper
1 cucumber, peeled and grated
4 lemon slices, to garnish

1. Pour the grapefruit juice into a saucepan. Add the gelatine and stir gently over a low heat until the gelatine has dissolved.
2. Add salt and pepper to taste and allow to cool.
3. As the grapefruit mixture begins to thicken, stir in the grated cucumber.
4. Allow the mixture to set in the refrigerator for about 2 hours.
5. To serve, roughly chop the jelly with a sharp knife and spoon into individual glasses. Garnish with lemon slices.

Above left: Jellied grapefruit and cucumber soup
Above right: Prawn and grapefruit cocktail
Bottom left: Stuffed tomatoes
Centre: Herbed cheese
Right: Cucumber mousse
Below: Stuffed curried eggs

STUFFED TOMATOES

Preparation time: 10 minutes
Cooking time: 20 minutes
KJ/calorie count: 420/100

4 large tomatoes
40 g/1½ oz brown rice
600 ml/1 pint stock
100 g/4 oz peas
1 small green pepper, cored, seeded and chopped
50 g/2 oz Edam or Cheshire cheese, finely chopped
1 teaspoon chopped fresh mint or ½ teaspoon dried mint
sprigs of mint, to garnish

1. Cut the tops off the tomatoes and scoop out the flesh from the centres.
2. Place the flesh in a saucepan with the rice and stock. Bring to the boil, then simmer for about 20 minutes until the rice is cooked but still firm. Drain and cool.
3. Cook the peas and pepper in boiling salted water for about 8 minutes, drain and cool.
4. Mix the rice, peas, pepper, cheese and mint together and spoon into the tomato shells. Garnish with sprigs of mint.

HERBED CHEESE

Preparation time: 5 minutes
KJ/calorie count: 330/80

225 g/8 oz curd or cottage cheese
2 teaspoons chopped fresh basil
2 teaspoons chopped fresh oregano
1 teaspoon mace
salt
freshly ground black pepper
mushroom caps, to serve

1. In a bowl, mix the cheese, herbs, mace, salt and pepper together with a fork.
2. Spoon the mixture into the mushroom caps for slimmers or serve with savoury biscuits for non-slimmers.
3. Alternatively, use sticks of raw vegetables such as carrot, green pepper and celery to dip in the mixture.

PRAWN & GRAPEFRUIT COCKTAIL

Preparation time: 10 minutes
KJ/calorie count: 440/105

2 grapefruit (preferably Florida)
350 g/12 oz peeled prawns
sprigs of mint, to garnish

This cocktail can be served with Aurora sauce – three parts low-calorie mayonnaise and one part tomato purée – but this adds another 130 calories!

1. Peel the grapefruit removing all the white pith. Cut between the membranes to remove the segments and cut each segment in half.
2. Mix the prawns and grapefruit together and spoon into individual glass dishes. Garnish with sprigs of mint.

VARIATION:
Substitute the grapefruit with small slices of melon, chopped.

STUFFED CURRIED EGGS

Preparation time: 10 minutes
KJ/calorie count: 420/100

6 hard-boiled eggs
3 tablespoons low-calorie
  mayonnaise
4 teaspoons curry paste
lettuce leaves

1. Cut the hardboiled eggs in half lengthways. Scoop out the yolks and mash with the mayonnaise and curry paste.
2. Spoon the mixture back into the whites and serve on lettuce leaves.

CUCUMBER MOUSSE

Preparation time: 10 minutes, plus
  chilling
KJ/calorie count: 420/100

1 large cucumber, finely chopped
225 g/8 oz curd cheese
150 ml/¼ pint plain unsweetened
  yogurt
pinch of mace
15 g/½ oz powdered gelatine
water
salt
freshly ground black pepper

1. Put the cucumber into a blender with the curd cheese, yogurt and mace.
2. Put the gelatine into a teacup of water, stand the cup in a bowl of hot water and stir until dissolved. Add the gelatine mixture to the blender.
3. Liquidize until the cucumber is thoroughly mixed into the cheese mixture.
4. Season to taste with salt and pepper, then turn into a soufflé dish or individual cocotte dishes and refrigerate, covered, overnight.

MACKEREL PÂTÉ

Preparation time: 5 minutes, plus chilling
KJ/calorie count: 710/170

1 × 225 g/8 oz can mackerel
4 rings fresh pineapple
1 tablespoon unsweetened pineapple juice
salt
freshly ground black pepper

1. Drain the canned mackerel well.
2. Put the fish, pineapple rings and pineapple juice in a blender and liquidize until smooth. Add salt and pepper to taste.
3. Spoon into individual cocotte dishes and chill in the refrigerator for 3 hours.

TUNA PÂTÉ

Preparation time: 10 minutes, plus setting
KJ/calorie count: 540/130

1 × 200 g/7 oz can tuna fish
250 ml/8 fl oz tomato juice
15 g/½ oz powdered gelatine
2 teaspoons chopped fresh basil or 1 teaspoon dried
2 teaspoons chopped fresh oregano or 1 teaspoon dried
salt
freshly ground black pepper

1. Thoroughly drain the oil from the can of tuna. Put the fish in a blender and add the tomato juice.
2. Put the gelatine in half a teacup of water, stand the cup in a bowl of hot water and stir until dissolved. Add the gelatine mixture to the mixture in the blender.
3. Liquidize until the mixture is fairly smooth. Add the herbs and salt and pepper and blend again until they are mixed in.
4. Turn into a dish and refrigerate for 4 hours until set.

SPANISH DIP WITH MUSHROOMS

Preparation time: 5 minutes, plus chilling
Cooking time: 15 minutes
KJ/calorie count: 170/40

225 g/8 oz tomatoes, skinned and chopped
1 large garlic clove, peeled and crushed
1 teaspoon chopped fresh oregano or ½ teaspoon dried oregano
4 tablespoons tomato juice
150 ml/¼ pint low-calorie mayonnaise
salt
freshly ground black pepper
raw button mushrooms, to serve

1. Put the tomatoes, garlic, oregano and tomato juice in a saucepan. Simmer gently for about 10 minutes until the mixture thickens and lightly coats the back of a spoon; reduce over a high heat if necessary.
2. Chill in the refrigerator for 3 hours.
3. When cold, stir in the mayonnaise. Taste and add salt and pepper if necessary. Serve with button mushrooms to dip.

CHICKEN LIVER PÂTÉ

Preparation time: 5 minutes, plus chilling
Cooking time: 5–8 minutes
KJ/calorie count: 380/90

225 g/8 oz chicken livers, trimmed
175 ml/6 fl oz tomato juice
1 garlic clove, crushed
1-2 teaspoons Worcestershire sauce
2 teaspoons chopped fresh basil or 1 teaspoon dried
2 teaspoons cream sherry
salt
freshly ground black pepper

1. Put the chicken livers in a non-stick frying pan with all the remaining ingredients. Simmer gently for 5-8 minutes until the livers are cooked on the outside but still pink inside.
2. Spoon the livers into a blender with a little of the cooking liquid and liquidize until smooth.
3. Spoon into individual cocotte dishes and refrigerate for about 4 hours before serving.

SALMON PÂTÉ

Preparation time: 10 minutes, plus chilling
KJ/calorie count: 500/120

200 g/7 oz cooked or canned salmon
150 ml/¼ pint plain unsweetened yogurt
1 teaspoon chopped fresh tarragon or ½ teaspoon dried
salt
freshly ground black pepper

1. If using canned salmon, drain it well. Skin and flake the fish using a fork. Put in a bowl and mash thoroughly.
2. Add the yogurt and stir until thoroughly mixed. Stir in the tarragon and salt and pepper to taste.
3. Chill in the refrigerator for about 2 hours before serving.

Above left: Chicken liver pâté
Above right: Spanish dip with mushrooms
Far left: Salmon pâté
Centre: Tuna pâté
Right: Mackerel pâté

QUICK & EASY

CHEESE WITH PRAWNS & ASPARAGUS

Preparation time: 10 minutes
KJ/calorie count: 750/180

450 g/1 lb cottage cheese
225 g/8 oz peeled prawns
salt
freshly ground black pepper
1 cucumber, peeled and diced
1 × 225 g/8 oz can asparagus
 spears, drained and chopped
lettuce leaves

1. Place the cottage cheese and prawns in a bowl and mix together. Add salt and pepper to taste. Stir in the cucumber and asparagus.
2. Make a bed of lettuce leaves on 4 plates.
3. Divide the mixture into 4 and spoon on to the lettuce.

KIDNEY BEAN SALAD

Preparation time: 10 minutes
KJ/calorie count: 840/200, plus
 dressing

1 × 425 g/15 oz can red kidney
 beans
175 g/6 oz Brie or Camembert
 cheese, cut into small pieces
100 g/4 oz onions, peeled and
 chopped
Lemon Vinaigrette (page 57), to
 serve

1. Drain the kidney beans thoroughly.
2. Mix the cheese, beans and onion together.
3. Serve with a Lemon Vinaigrette.

CHEESE-STUFFED PEARS

Preparation time: 10 minutes, plus
 chilling
KJ/calorie count: about 840/200

275 g/10 oz curd cheese
25 g/1 oz walnuts, chopped
1 teaspoon ground ginger or
 mixed spice
salt
freshly ground black pepper
4 ripe medium pears, halved and
 cored

1. Mix the curd cheese, walnuts and spice together. Add salt and pepper to taste.
2. Pile into the pear cavities and chill before serving.

Top left: Cheese with prawns
and asparagus
Top right: Kidney bean salad
Bottom: Cheese-stuffed pears

BAKED PILCHARD LOAF

Preparation time: 15 minutes
Cooking time: 20 minutes
KJ/calorie count: each slice about 840/
   200

225 g/8 oz canned pilchards,
   drained
50 g/2 oz tomato purée
75 g/3 oz low-calorie spread
1 teaspoon chopped fresh parsley
salt
freshly ground black pepper
1 small white loaf

1. Mash together the pilchards, tomato purée and low-calorie spread. Add the parsley and salt and pepper.
2. Make about 8 diagonal cuts in the loaf and spread each cut side with the pilchard mixture.
3. Wrap the loaf in kitchen foil and place in a preheated oven at 200°C, 400°F, Gas Mark 6 for about 20 minutes.
4. Fold back the foil for the last 5 minutes of cooking time to allow the crust to become crisp.

MARINATED MACKEREL

Preparation time: 15 minutes, plus
   marinating
KJ/calorie count: 1250/300

4 smoked mackerel fillets
Curry Vinaigrette (page 56)
lettuce leaves
apple slices, to garnish

1. Skin the mackerel and remove any bones..
2. Flake the flesh, place in the curry vinaigrette and leave to marinate for 3 hours.
3. Line 4 individual serving dishes with lettuce leaves. Spoon the mackerel on to the lettuce.
4. Garnish with slices of apple and serve immediately.

BAKED TOMATOES

Preparation time: 10 minutes
Cooking time: 10–15 minutes
*KJ/calorie count: 670/160 per tomato
    half*

2 large tomatoes, halved
100 g/4 oz wholemeal
    breadcrumbs
100 g/4 oz lean ham, diced
100 g/4 oz cooked peas
2 teaspoons tomato purée
salt
freshly ground black pepper

Choose large tomatoes weighing about
225 g/8 oz for these recipes. If unavailable
use smaller tomatoes, cutting off the tops
and using them whole, not cut into halves.
Use 4 smaller tomatoes to one large one.

1. Scoop out the tomato flesh with a
teaspoon. Mash the flesh and stir in the
breadcrumbs, ham, peas, tomato purée
and salt and pepper to taste.
2. Divide the mixture into 4 and spoon
into the tomato halves.
3. Place in an ovenproof dish and bake in
a preheated oven at 200°C, 400°F, Gas
Mark 6 for 10-15 minutes. It may be
necessary to cover the tops of the tomatoes
towards the end of the cooking time to
prevent burning. Serve hot or cold.

VARIATIONS:
Use 100 g/4 oz grated cheese instead of
ham.
KJ/calorie count: 840/200
Use 100 g/4 oz flaked canned tuna fish
instead of ham.
KJ/calorie count: 585/140
Use 100 g/4 oz peeled prawns instead of
ham.
KJ/calorie count: 500/120

**Above left: Baked pilchard loaf
Above right: Marinated
mackerel
Below left: Baked tomatoes
Centre: Courgette cheese pie
Below right: Cheese pudding**

COURGETTE CHEESE PIE

Preparation time: 10 minutes
Cooking time: about 40 minutes
KJ/calorie count: 1045/250

8 courgettes, thinly sliced
225 g/8 oz mature Cheddar or
    Gruyère cheese, grated
salt
freshly ground black pepper

1. Place a layer of courgette slices on the
base of a casserole dish, adding salt and
pepper to taste.
2. Sprinkle a layer of cheese on top of the
courgettes. Repeat the layers until the
courgettes and cheese are used up,
finishing with cheese.
3. Sprinkle salt and pepper on top. Cover
the casserole and bake in a preheated oven
at 180°C, 350°F, Gas Mark 4 for about 35
minutes or until the courgettes are soft.
4. Uncover and place under a preheated
hot grill for a few minutes to brown the
cheese.

CHEESE PUDDING

Preparation time: 10 minutes
Cooking time: 30 minutes
KJ/calorie count: 1670/400

6 slices bread
made mustard
175 g/6 oz cheese, grated
600 ml/1 pint skimmed milk
3 eggs, beaten
salt
freshly ground black pepper

1. Spread the bread slices with mustard.
2. Arrange a layer of bread on the base of
a soufflé dish. Sprinkle over a layer of
cheese and repeat the layers until the
bread and cheese are used up, finishing
with cheese.
3. Add the milk to the eggs and beat
together. Add salt and pepper, then pour
the mixture over the bread and cheese.
4. Bake in a preheated oven at 180°C,
350°F, Gas Mark 4 for about 30 minutes.

PIPÉRADE

Preparation time: 10 minutes
Cooking time: about 15 minutes
KJ/calorie count: 460/110

2 tablespoons tomato juice
1 large red pepper, cored, seeded and sliced
100 g/4 oz onions, peeled and sliced
4 tomatoes, sliced
1 teaspoon dried oregano
salt
freshly ground black pepper
4 eggs, beaten

1. Put the tomato juice in a non-stick saucepan. Add the sliced red pepper and onions and cook for about 5 minutes until soft.
2. Add the tomatoes and cook gently for 5 minutes. If necessary, add more tomato juice but the mixture should be fairly thick.
3. Stir the oregano and salt and pepper into the beaten eggs. Add the eggs to the mixture, raise the heat slightly and cook quickly, stirring continuously.
4. Spoon on to a heated serving plate.

HAM & MUSTARD

Serves 1
Preparation time: 5 minutes
KJ/calorie count: 940/225

low-calorie spread
1 slice brown bread
40 g/1½ oz cooked ham without fat
25 g/1 oz Gruyère or Edam cheese, diced
½ teaspoon made mustard

1. Spread the fat lightly on the bread.
2. Place the ham on top of the bread.
3. Mix the cheese and mustard together and pile on top of the ham.

Right: Pipérade
Far right: Ham and mustard

BUCK RAREBIT

Preparation time: 10 minutes
Cooking time: 10 minutes
KJ/calorie count: 1250/300

4 eggs
4 slices bread
4 slices Gruyère cheese

1. To poach the eggs, half fill a frying pan with water, adding a pinch of salt or a few drops of vinegar.
2. Bring the water to the boil, break the eggs and gently slide them into the water. Cook gently until lightly set.
3. Meanwhile, toast the bread under a preheated grill on one side only.
4. Place the cheese on the untoasted sides of the bread and return to the grill to brown.
5. Remove the poached eggs from the water, drain, and trim the whites.
6. Place on the toasted cheese slice and serve immediately.

BAKED EGGS WITH PEPPERS

Preparation time: 10 minutes
Cooking time: 25 minutes
KJ/calorie count: 1130/270

3 red peppers, cored, seeded and thinly sliced
1 medium onion, peeled and thinly sliced
250 ml/8 fl oz tomato juice
120 ml/4 fl oz chicken stock
dash of Worcestershire sauce
4 eggs

1. Place the peppers and onion in a saucepan with the tomato juice, chicken stock and Worcestershire sauce. Cook gently for about 10 minutes until the peppers are almost soft.
2. Transfer the mixture to a shallow casserole or earthenware dish. Make 4 hollows and gently break an egg into each.
3. Bake in a preheated oven at 200°C, 400°F, Gas Mark 6 for 10-15 minutes until the eggs are set.

Right: Baked eggs with peppers
Centre: Oeufs en cocotte
Far right: Buck rarebit

OEUFS EN COCOTTE

Preparation time: 5 minutes
Cooking time: 10-15 minutes
KJ/calorie count: 330/80

15 g/½ oz butter
4 eggs
salt
freshly ground black pepper
4 teaspoons curd cheese

1. Smear the bottom and sides of 4 ovenproof cocotte dishes with butter.
2. Break an egg carefully into each dish and add salt and pepper.
3. Place the dishes in a roasting tin with water to come halfway up the sides of the dishes. Place a teaspoon of curd cheese on top of each egg.
4. Bake in a preheated oven at 200°C, 400°F, Gas Mark 6 for 10-15 minutes according to how you like the eggs set.

VARIATIONS:
Place 15 g/½ oz chopped lean cooked ham in the bottom of the cocotte dishes before breaking in the eggs
KJ/calorie count: 460/110
Add asparagus tips
KJ/calorie count: 20/5 per 25 g/1 oz
Add diced chicken
KJ/calorie count: 230/55 per 25 g/ 1 oz
Sprinkle grated cheese on top
KJ/calorie count: 420/100 per 25 g/1 oz

Feather pancakes
From the top: Spinach and cheese; Ratatouille; Cheese and raisin; Smoked haddock

FEATHER PANCAKES

Preparation time: 5 minutes, plus chilling
Cooking time: about 2 minutes per pancake
KJ/calorie count: 250-270/60-65 per pancake

1 tablespoon plain flour
salt
1 egg
300 ml/½ pint skimmed milk
knob of butter (optional)

1. Place the flour and salt in a bowl and make a well in the centre. Break in the egg and add the milk.
2. Beat with a whisk until well blended. Chill the batter for 2-3 hours.
3. Use a non-stick frying pan about 18 cm/7 inches in diameter. Melt a little butter in the pan and pour in about a quarter of the batter.
4. Move the pan to allow the batter to spread evenly. Cook for 1-2 minutes until lightly browned on the underside. Toss the pancake or turn over using a spatula and brown the other side.
5. Slide the pancake on to a heated plate or dish and place in a warm oven. Repeat the process to make the other three pancakes.

PANCAKE FILLINGS:
Although pancakes are delicious served with lemon juice and sugar alone, KJ/calorie count: 80/20 per 1 teaspoon sugar, they can also be filled with other ingredients to make a more substantial dish.

SPINACH & CHEESE FILLING

Preparation time: 5 minutes
KJ/calorie count: 540/130

350 g/12 oz cooked chopped spinach
100 g/4 oz cheese, grated
salt
freshly ground black pepper

1. Mix the spinach and cheese together, add salt and pepper to taste and divide into 4.
2. Spoon the filling on to each pancake and fold over.

RATATOUILLE FILLING

Preparation time: 15 minutes
Cooking time: about 20 minutes
KJ/calorie count: 500/120

Ratatouille (page 109)

1. Make the ratatouille mixture and divide into 4.
2. Spoon on to each pancake and fold over.

CHEESE & RAISIN FILLING

Preparation time: 5 minutes
KJ/calorie count: 710/170

100 g/4 oz raisins
275 g/10 oz curd cheese

1. Mix the raisins and curd cheese together and divide into 4.
2. Spoon the filling on to each pancake and fold over.

SMOKED HADDOCK FILLING

Preparation time: 5 minutes
Cooking time: 2 minutes
KJ/calorie count: 460/110

225 g/8 oz smoked haddock, cooked and flaked
2 hard-boiled eggs, chopped
50 ml/2 fl oz single cream
salt
freshly ground black pepper

1. Put the flaked haddock, chopped eggs and cream into a saucepan.
2. Stir over a gentle heat until warmed through, but do not let the mixture boil. Add salt and pepper to taste and divide the mixture into 4.
3. Spoon the filling on to each pancake and fold over.

PLAIN OMELETTE

Serves 1
Preparation time: 5 minutes
Cooking time: 2-3 minutes
KJ/calorie count: 750/180

2 eggs
1 dessertspoon top of the milk or
     water
salt
freshly ground black pepper
knob of butter

Omelettes are a low-calorie, quick and easy meal. There are many ways to vary omelettes; try adding chopped fresh herbs, tomato, cheese or make a filling Spanish omelette.

1. Beat the eggs together lightly and add the top of the milk or water and salt and pepper.
2. Melt the butter in a non-stick omelette or small frying pan and pour in the egg mixture. As the omelette begins to set underneath, tilt the pan to let the liquid egg run to the side of the pan.
3. The omelette is cooked when the centre is still creamy. Fold the omelette over with a palette knife and slide it on to a heated plate. Do not overcook omelettes as they will toughen.

Below left: Tomato omelette
Centre: Cheese omelette
Right: Spanish omelette

VARIATIONS:

SPANISH OMELETTE
To the plain omelette mixture add 100 g/ 4 oz cooked mixed vegetables, e.g. peas, carrots, potatoes, onions, as it begins to set. Serve open.
KJ/calorie count: 210/50 for the filling

CHEESE & PEPPER OMELETTE
Add 1 finely chopped green pepper to the eggs (optional) and sprinkle 40 g/1½ oz grated Cheddar or Gruyère cheese over the cooked omelette.
KJ/calorie count: 750/180 for the filling

TOMATO OMELETTE
Add 1 medium skinned, chopped tomato to the omelette mixture as it begins to set.
KJ/calorie count: 64/16 for the filling
Alternatively, add 25 g/1 oz tomato purée to the beaten eggs, making sure it is fully blended before cooking the egg mixture.
KJ/calorie count: 65/16 for the filling

BAKED POTATOES

KJ/calorie count per 100 g/4 oz potato:
420/100

Potatoes should not be ignored on a slimming regime – they are both nutritious and satisfying, and with a filling can make a balanced, easy to prepare meal.

If baking more than one potato, choose even sized ones. Scrub, dry and prick all over with a fork. Place on a baking sheet and bake in a preheated oven at 200°C, 400°F, Gas Mark 6 for 1-1¼ hours until tender when pierced with a knife. Add one of the following fillings, or for an informal supper, make up all these fillings and let guests choose their own. Serve with soup and salad.

BLUE CHEESE FILLING

Preparation time: 5 minutes
Cooking time: 2 minutes, plus baking potato
KJ/calorie count: Danish blue 880/210 excluding potato; Stilton: 1250/300 excluding potato

FOR EACH POTATO:
50 g/2 oz blue cheese, use Danish or Stilton
4 teaspoons plain unsweetened yogurt
salt
freshly ground black pepper

1. Crumble the cheese into the yogurt and add salt and pepper to taste.
2. Cut a cross in the top of the potato and spoon on the cheese and yogurt mixture.
3. Return to the oven for about 2 minutes to heat through. Serve on lettuce.

CAMEMBERT FILLING

Preparation time: 10 minutes
Cooking time: 2 minutes, plus baking potato
KJ/calorie count: 840/200 excluding potato

FOR EACH POTATO:
50 g/2 oz Camembert cheese
50 g/2 oz cottage cheese
salt
freshly ground black pepper

1. Remove the rind from the Camembert and mash with the cottage cheese and salt and pepper using a wooden spoon.
2. Cut the potato in half, scoop out the flesh from the skins and combine with the cheese mixture.
3. Spoon back into the potato shells. Place under the grill or return to the oven for about 2 minutes to heat through. Serve with salad.

COTTAGE CHEESE FILLING

Preparation time: 10 minutes
Cooking time: 2 minutes, plus baking potato
KJ/calorie count: 230/55 excluding potato

FOR EACH POTATO:
50 g/2 oz cottage cheese
2 teaspoons tomato purée
salt
freshly ground black pepper

1. Mix the cottage cheese, tomato purée and salt and pepper together.
2. Cut the potato in half, scoop out the flesh from the skins and combine with the cheese and tomato mixture.
3. Spoon back into the potato shells. Return to the oven for 2 minutes to heat through.

Above: Baked potatoes, from top left: Cottage cheese filling; Blue cheese filling; Camembert filling

Right: Stuffed eggs, from the left: Sardine and mayonnaise filling; Devilled cheese filling; Haddock and mayonnaise filling

STUFFED EGGS

Hard-boiled eggs can be stuffed with a number of interesting fillings. They are excellent for a packed meal, to take on a picnic, or simply served with a salad.

SARDINE & MAYONNAISE FILLING

Preparation time: 10 minutes
KJ/calorie count: 630/150 per stuffed egg

4 hard-boiled eggs, halved
1 × 100 g/4 oz can sardines, drained
1 dessertspoon low-calorie mayonnaise
salt
freshly ground black pepper

1. Remove the yolks from the eggs.
2. Mix the yolks, sardines and mayonnaise together. Add salt and pepper to taste.
3. Pile the mixture into the egg halves.

DEVILLED CHEESE FILLING

Preparation time: 10 minutes
KJ/calorie count: 540/130 per stuffed egg

4 hard-boiled eggs, halved
50 g/2 oz Cheddar cheese, finely grated
2 dessertspoons low-calorie mayonnaise
1 teaspoon Worcestershire sauce
1 teaspoon made mustard
freshly ground black pepper

1. Remove the yolks from the eggs.
2. Mix the yolks, grated cheese, mayonnaise, Worcestershire sauce and mustard together. Add salt and pepper to taste.
3. Pile the mixture into the egg halves.

HADDOCK & MAYONNAISE FILLING

Preparation time: 10 minutes
KJ/calorie count: 500/120 per stuffed egg

4 hard-boiled eggs, halved
100 g/4 oz smoked haddock, cooked and flaked
1 dessertspoon low-calorie mayonnaise
cayenne pepper, to taste

1. Remove the yolks from the eggs.
2. Mix the yolks, haddock, mayonnaise and cayenne pepper together.
3. Pile the mixture into the egg halves.

TUNA & GRAPEFRUIT CUPS

Preparation time: 15 minutes
KJ/calorie count: 1250/300

2 large grapefruit
2 × 200 g/7 oz cans tuna fish, drained
1 cucumber, peeled and diced
4 sticks celery, chopped
1 dessert apple, cored and cut into slices
salt
freshly ground black pepper
lettuce leaves (optional)

1. Cut the grapefruit in half and remove the flesh by cutting between the membranes. Reserve the grapefruit shells.
2. Mix the grapefruit pulp with the tuna fish. Stir in the cucumber, celery, apple, and salt and pepper to taste.
3. Divide the mixture into 4 and pile into the grapefruit shells or arrange on lettuce leaves.

EGG & PRAWN SALAD

Preparation time: 10 minutes
KJ/calorie count: 920/220

225 g/8 oz peeled prawns
100 g/4 oz petits pois, cooked
2 tablespoons low-calorie mayonnaise
salt
freshly ground black pepper
cayenne pepper (optional)
4 hard-boiled eggs, sliced
4 teaspoons lumpfish roe (optional)

1. Mix the prawns, petits pois and mayonnaise together in a bowl. Add salt and pepper and a pinch of cayenne pepper, if liked.
2. Arrange the egg slices on 4 plates.
3. Spoon over the prawn mixture and top with the lumpfish roe if used.

SCRAMBLED EGGS WITH SMOKED HADDOCK

Preparation time: 5 minutes
Cooking time: about 20 minutes
KJ/calorie count: 1045/250

450 g/1 lb smoked haddock
knob of butter
8 eggs, beaten
salt
freshly ground black pepper

1. Poach the haddock in the minimum of water for about 15 minutes until tender. Drain and flake the haddock with a fork. Keep warm.
2. Melt the butter in a non-stick pan. Pour in the eggs, stirring.
3. As the eggs start to set, add the haddock and a little salt and pepper and stir continuously. When cooked, serve immediately with plenty of black pepper.

CHEESE & TOMATO TOAST

Preparation time: 10 minutes
Cooking time: 15 minutes
KJ/calorie count: 1045/250

4 slices bread
175 g/6 oz cheese, grated
4 teaspoons tomato purée
4 small tomatoes, sliced

1. Toast the bread under the grill on one side only.
2. Mix the cheese and tomato purée together. Spread on to the untoasted sides of the bread.
3. Return to the grill and, when the mixture is bubbling, place the sliced tomatoes on top.
4. Grill until the tomatoes soften.

From the top: Tuna and grapefruit cups; Egg and prawn salad; Scrambled eggs with smoked haddock; Cheese and tomato toast

OPEN SANDWICHES

The ingredients are given for 1 open sandwich. You may use any type of bread you like, lightly spread with a low-calorie spread or mayonnaise (if an ingredient).

ASPARAGUS & CRAB

Preparation time: 5 minutes
KJ/calorie count: 670/160

low-calorie spread
1 slice rye bread
4 canned asparagus spears
75 g/3 oz crab meat
1 slice lemon, to garnish

1. Spread the fat lightly on the bread.
2. Arrange the asparagus spears on half the slice and trim as necessary.
3. Flake the crab meat with a fork and spoon on to the other half of the bread. Garnish with the lemon.

SALAMI & EGG

Preparation time: 5 minutes
KJ/calorie count: 1380/330

low-calorie spread
1 slice granary bread
40 g/1½ oz salami
1 gherkin, sliced
2 slices hard-boiled egg
1 onion ring

1. Spread the fat lightly on the bread, then cover with the salami.
2. Top with the sliced gherkin, hard-boiled egg and onion ring.

SARDINE & CUCUMBER

Preparation time: 5 minutes
KJ/calorie count: 1045/250

low-calorie spread
1 slice granary bread
lettuce leaf
8 slices cucumber
75 g/3 oz canned sardines, drained

1. Spread the fat lightly on the bread.
2. Arrange the lettuce leaf and cucumber slices on the bread. Place the sardines on top.

VARIATION:
Use shrimps instead of sardines.
KJ/calorie count: 460/110

PEAR & HAM

Preparation time: 5 minutes
KJ/calorie count: 840/200

low-calorie spread
1 slice wholemeal bread
25 g/1 oz prosciutto or Parma ham
½ ripe pear, peeled, cored and cubed

1. Spread the fat lightly on the bread.
2. Place the ham in curls on the bread. Pile the pear cubes on top.

BLUE CHEESE

Preparation time: 5 minutes
KJ/calorie count: 750/180

1 slice rye bread
1 tablespoon low-calorie mayonnaise
25 g/1 oz blue cheese
chicory leaves
1 slice orange, to garnish

1. Spread the bread with a little of the mayonnaise. Crumble the blue cheese into the remaining mayonnaise and mix well.
2. Arrange the chicory leaves on the bread and pile the blue cheese mixture on top. Garnish with the orange.

Open sandwiches, from the top: Asparagus and crab; Salami and egg; Sardine and cucumber; Pear and ham; Blue cheese

SALADS

CHEESE, APRICOT & WALNUT SALAD

Preparation time: 15 minutes
KJ/calorie count: 730/175, plus dressing

8 apricots, skinned
4 tablespoons curd cheese or cottage cheese
100 g/4 oz walnuts, chopped
salt
freshly ground black pepper

TO GARNISH:
lettuce leaves
1 dessertspoon chopped fresh tarragon
Orange Vinaigrette (page 57), to serve

1. Halve the apricots and remove the stones with a small sharp knife.
2. Mix the curd cheese or cottage cheese with the walnuts, season to taste with salt and pepper, then spoon into the hollows of the apricots.
3. Arrange on lettuce leaves and sprinkle with the tarragon. Serve with an Orange Vinaigrette.

CARROT & ORANGE SALAD

Preparation time: 15 minutes
KJ/calorie count: 420/100, plus dressing

2 large carrots, scraped
4 oranges
1 head of chicory
lettuce leaves
Orange Vinaigrette (page 57), to serve

1. Grate the carrots coarsely.
2. Peel and discard the skin and pith from the oranges, then slice the flesh thinly into rounds, removing all the pips.
3. Slice the chicory thinly.
4. Arrange the lettuce on a shallow serving dish and attractively arrange the grated carrot and orange and chicory slices on top. Serve with an Orange Vinaigrette.

MUSHROOM CABBAGE SLAW

Preparation time: 15 minutes, plus chilling
KJ/calorie count: 310/75

225 g/8 oz mushrooms
225 g/8 oz white cabbage
50 g/2 oz sultanas
300 ml/½ pint plain unsweetened yogurt
2 tablespoons lemon juice
2 tablespoons Dijon mustard
salt
freshly ground black pepper
2 tablespoons chopped fresh chives

1. Slice the mushrooms thinly and shred the cabbage.
2. Mix the mushrooms, cabbage and sultanas together in a bowl.
3. Stir the yogurt, lemon juice, mustard, salt and pepper together. Pour over the mushroom mixture and mix well.
4. Cover the bowl and chill overnight.
5. Stir before serving then sprinkle with the chives.

Top: Cheese, apricot and walnut salad
Left: Carrot and orange salad
Right: Mushroom cabbage slaw

GREEN SALAD

Preparation time: 10 minutes
KJ/calorie count: 100/25, plus
   dressing

1 small lettuce
100 g/4 oz spinach, stalks removed
½ curly endive
½ cucumber
8 spring onions, trimmed
1 garlic clove, peeled and crushed
Lemon Vinaigrette (page 57)
1 tablespoon chopped fresh
   tarragon and thyme, to garnish

1. Line a deep salad bowl with lettuce leaves. Shred the remaining lettuce with the spinach and endive and place in the bowl.
2. Thinly slice the cucumber, chop the spring onions and scatter them over the top.
3. Just before serving, mix the crushed garlic clove with a little Lemon Vinaigrette and toss with the salad. Garnish with the tarragon and thyme.

Left, from the top: Green salad;
Bean, tomato and pepper salad;
Neapolitan salad; Greek salad
Right, from the top: Tomato and
anchovy salad; Salad niçoise

BEAN, TOMATO & PEPPER SALAD

Preparation time: 15 minutes
Cooking time: 12 minutes
KJ/calorie count: 100/25, plus
   dressing

225 g/8 oz French beans
4 large tomatoes, skinned
1 large red pepper, cored, seeded
   and sliced
1 dessertspoon chopped fresh
   basil or oregano, to garnish
Lemon Vinaigrette (page 57)

1. Cook the beans in boiling salted water for about 12 minutes until tender. Drain and cool.
2. Cut the tomatoes into quarters.
3. Blanch the pepper in boiling water for 1 minute. Drain.
4. Cut the beans in half and place in a serving dish with the tomato and pepper. Mix together and sprinkle with the basil or oregano. Serve with a Lemon Vinaigrette.

NEAPOLITAN SALAD

Preparation time: 10 minutes
Cooking time: 10 minutes
KJ/calorie count: 880/210, plus
   dressing

100 g/4 oz shell pasta
100 g/4 oz canned tuna fish
4 tomatoes, skinned
1 medium onion, peeled and
   chopped
1 teaspoon chopped fresh
   oregano, to garnish
Yogurt and Lemon Dressing
   (page 57)

1. Simmer the pasta in boiling salted water for about 10 minutes until just cooked but still firm. Drain and cool.
2. Drain the oil from the tuna and separate the fish into bite-sized pieces.
3. Cut the tomatoes into quarters.
4. Mix the pasta, tuna, tomatoes and onion together in a salad bowl and sprinkle with the oregano. Serve with a Yogurt and Lemon Dressing.

GREEK SALAD

Preparation time: 15 minutes
KJ/calorie count: 1250/300, plus
   dressing

1 Cos lettuce
½ cucumber, peeled
4 tomatoes, skinned
8 spring onions, trimmed
1 × 50 g/2 oz can anchovy fillets
1 dessertspoon chopped fresh
   basil or 1 teaspoon dried basil
225 g/8 oz Feta cheese
Lemon Vinaigrette (page 57)

If you cannot buy Feta cheese, Wensleydale is a good substitute.

1. Shred the lettuce and arrange on a large platter or shallow serving dish.
2. Cut the cucumber into 2.5 cm/1 inch lengths and arrange on top of the lettuce.
3. Slice the tomatoes thinly and arrange round the edge of the platter.
4. Chop the spring onions. Drain the oil from the anchovies and cut them into small pieces. Sprinkle the spring onion,

anchovy and basil over the salad.
5. Cut the Feta cheese into small dice and pile on top of the salad. Serve with a Lemon Vinaigrette.

TOMATO & ANCHOVY SALAD

Preparation time: 10 minutes
*KJ/calorie count: 290/70, plus
    dressing*

4 large tomatoes, skinned
1 large red pepper, cored, seeded
    and thinly sliced
1 × 50 g/2 oz can anchovies
Lemon Vinaigrette (page 57)

1. Slice the tomatoes thinly.
2. Blanch the pepper in boiling water for 1 minute. Drain.
3. Drain the oil from the anchovies, rinse carefully and dry them.
4. On a flat serving plate, arrange the tomato slices and pepper rings in an attractive pattern. Lay the anchovies over

them in a trellis pattern. Serve with a Lemon Vinaigrette.

SALAD NIÇOISE

Preparation time: 15 minutes
Cooking time: 20 minutes
*KJ/calorie count: 1380/330, plus
    dressing*

lettuce leaves
3 medium potatoes
225 g/8 oz French beans
4 tomatoes, skinned
2 hard-boiled eggs
1 × 225 g/8 oz can tuna fish
1 × 50 g/2 oz can anchovies
Lemon Vinaigrette (page 57)

This salad will serve as a light main course.

1. Arrange the lettuce leaves on a serving dish.
2. Cook the potatoes in boiling salted water for 15-20 minutes. Drain and cool, then skin and dice.
3. Meanwhile, cook the French beans in boiling salted water for about 12 minutes. Drain and cool, then chop roughly.
4. Chop the tomatoes and eggs roughly.
5. Drain the oil from the tuna and separate the fish into bite-sized pieces. Drain the oil

from the anchovies and chop roughly.
6. Mix all the ingredients together and pile on to the bed of lettuce. Serve with a Lemon Vinaigrette.

CURRIED MUSHROOM SALAD

Preparation time: 15 minutes, plus chilling
KJ/calorie count: 920/220

500 g/1 lb button mushrooms
½ cucumber, peeled
225 g/8 oz cooked ham
300 ml/½ pint plain unsweetened yogurt
about 2 teaspoons curry paste
4 teaspoons lemon juice
salt
freshly ground black pepper

1. Cut the larger mushrooms into quarters.
2. Dice the cucumber and cut the ham into bite-sized pieces.
3. Stir the mushrooms, ham and cucumber together in a bowl.
4. Mix the yogurt, curry paste and lemon juice together. Chill both mixtures for 1 hour.
5. Combine the mushroom and yogurt mixtures together, adding salt and pepper to taste. Chill for a further hour before serving.

FRESH BEETROOT SALAD

Preparation time: about 15 minutes, plus chilling
KJ/calorie count: 355/85

1 dessertspoon olive oil
1 dessertspoon lemon juice
1 teaspoon made mustard
3-4 small uncooked beetroots, peeled and coarsely grated
1 cucumber, peeled and sliced
1 tablespoon chopped fresh mixed herbs

1. Mix the olive oil, lemon juice and mustard together. Stir into the beetroot.
2. Arrange the cucumber slices round the edge of a shallow dish.
3. Put the beetroot mixture in the centre. Scatter over the herbs. Chill before serving.

Top: Curried mushroom salad
Left: Fresh beetroot salad
Centre: Apple, celery and cheese salad
Right: Mixed vegetable salad

MIXED VEGETABLE SALAD

Preparation time: 15 minutes
Cooking time: about 20 minutes
KJ/calorie count: 440/105, plus dressing

4 carrots, peeled
225 g/8 oz potatoes, peeled
salt
225 g/8 oz peas
225 g/8 oz shelled broad beans
Lemon Vinaigrette (page 57), to serve

1. Dice the carrots and potatoes. Cook in boiling salted water for about 10 minutes until just cooked but still firm.
2. Meanwhile, cook the peas in boiling salted water for 6-12 minutes, depending on whether frozen or fresh, until tender.
3. Cook the broad beans in boiling salted water for about 15 minutes until tender.
4. Mix all the vegetables together in a salad bowl. This salad may be eaten hot or cold. Serve with a Lemon Vinaigrette.

BROAD BEAN SALAD

Preparation time: 10 minutes
KJ/calorie count: 420/100, plus dressing

225 g/8 oz young spinach, trimmed
450 g/1 lb cooked broad beans
100 g/4 oz cooked peas
4 tomatoes, sliced
Lemon Vinaigrette (page 57), to serve

1. Shred the spinach leaves. Arrange in a serving dish.
2. Mix the beans and peas together and place in the centre of the spinach.
3. Arrange the tomato slices around the beans. Serve with a Lemon Vinaigrette.

Left: Broad bean salad
Right: Cole slaw

APPLE, CELERY & CHEESE SALAD

Preparation time: 10 minutes
KJ/calorie count: Cheddar cheese –
1170/280; Gruyère cheese – 1250/
300, plus dressing

---

4 eating apples, Cox's Orange
 Pippins preferably
lemon juice
4 sticks celery, trimmed
225 g/8 oz Cheddar or Gruyère
 cheese
Lemon Vinaigrette (page 57), to
 serve

1. Core the apples, cut into bite-sized
pieces and dip in lemon juice to prevent
discoloration.
2. Chop the celery and dice the cheese.
3. Mix all the ingredients together in a
salad bowl. Non-slimmers can add a
handful of chopped walnuts. Serve with a
Lemon Vinaigrette.

COLE SLAW

Preparation time: 20 minutes, plus
soaking
KJ/calorie count: 170/40

---

1 firm white cabbage (about 450 g/
 1 lb), grated
100 g/4 oz carrot, peeled and
 grated
1 medium onion, peeled and
 sliced
Yogurt and Lemon Dressing
 (page 57)

1. Plunge the grated cabbage in cold
salted water for at least 1 hour, longer if
possible. Drain thoroughly and pat dry.
2. Mix the cabbage, carrot and onion
together in a large bowl.
3. Stir in the Yogurt and Lemon Dressing.

BEETROOT & HORSERADISH SALAD

Preparation time: 10 minutes
KJ/calorie count: 500/120

2 heads of chicory
4 medium cooked beetroots,
    peeled and diced
2 tablespoons low-calorie
    mayonnaise
2 teaspoons grated horseradish
1 teaspoon mustard powder

1. Line a serving dish with the chicory leaves. Spoon the beetroot in the centre.
2. Mix the mayonnaise, horseradish and mustard together and spoon on top of the beetroot.

FENNEL SALAD

Preparation time: 15 minutes
KJ/calorie count: 290/70, plus
*   dressing*

2 eating apples, Cox's Orange
    Pippins preferably
lemon juice
2 fennel bulbs, trimmed
4 sticks celery, trimmed
salt
freshly ground black pepper
chopped spring onion, to garnish
Lemon Vinaigrette (page 57), to
    serve

1. Core the apples, cut into slices and dip in lemon juice to prevent discoloration. Place in a serving dish.
2. Slice the fennel and celery and mix with the apple and salt and pepper. Garnish with chopped spring onion. Serve with a Lemon Vinaigrette.

Left: Beetroot and
horseradish salad
Centre: Fennel salad
Right: Orange and
dandelion salad

EGG & CUCUMBER SALAD

Preparation time: 15 minutes
KJ/calorie count: 500/120

1 bunch watercress
1 cucumber, peeled and sliced
4 hard-boiled eggs, finely chopped
1 bunch spring onions, chopped

SAUCE:
300 ml/½ pint plain unsweetened
    yogurt
1 tablespoon lemon juice
1 teaspoon mustard powder
salt
freshly ground black pepper

1. Arrange the watercress in a serving dish and cover with the cucumber slices.
2. Mix the chopped eggs and spring onions together and spoon into the centre.
3. To make the sauce, mix all the ingredients together. Pour over the salad and serve.

BEAN SPROUT SALAD

Preparation time: 10 minutes
KJ/calorie count: 100/25

225 g/8 oz bean sprouts
1 red pepper, cored, seeded and
    chopped
½ cucumber, peeled and chopped
1 dessertspoon chopped fresh
    chives
salt
freshly ground black pepper
2 teaspoons soy sauce

1. Place the bean sprouts in a salad bowl.
2. Stir in the chopped red pepper and cucumber.
3. Add the chives and salt and pepper to taste just before serving, mixing well. Sprinkle with the soy sauce.

Left: Bean sprout salad
Centre: Golden salad
Right: Egg and cucumber salad

ORANGE & DANDELION SALAD

Preparation time: 10 minutes
KJ/calorie count: 210/50, plus
dressing

450 g/1 lb young dandelion leaves
2 oranges, sliced and quartered
1 bunch watercress
50 g/2 oz spring onions, chopped
Orange Vinaigrette (page 57), to
serve

1. Shred the dandelion leaves and pile into a serving dish.
2. Arrange the orange slices and watercress on top. Scatter over the chopped spring onions. Serve with an Orange Vinaigrette.

VARIATION:
Use curly endive or young spinach leaves instead of dandelion leaves.

GOLDEN SALAD

Preparation time: 10 minutes
KJ/calorie count: 380/90, plus
dressing

lettuce leaves
450 g/1 lb Jerusalem artichokes,
    cooked and sliced
wine vinegar
pinch of ground mace
4 hard-boiled eggs
Lemon or Orange Vinaigrette
    (page 57), to serve

1. Line a salad bowl with lettuce leaves.
2. Arrange the sliced artichokes on top of the lettuce. Sprinkle with a little vinegar to keep them white. Add the mace.
3. Sieve the egg yolks and chop the whites, then scatter over the lettuce and artichokes. Serve with a Lemon or Orange Vinaigrette.

COURGETTES & YOGURT

Preparation time: 10 minutes
KJ/calorie count: 310/75

8 small courgettes, peeled
lemon juice
300 ml/½ pint plain unsweetened
    yogurt
salt
freshly ground black pepper

1. Thinly slice or grate the courgettes.
2. Mix enough lemon juice into the yogurt to make a fluid consistency. Add salt and pepper to taste.
3. Mix the courgettes and yogurt together. Serve with a curry.

VARIATION:
Use 1 medium cucumber instead of courgettes.

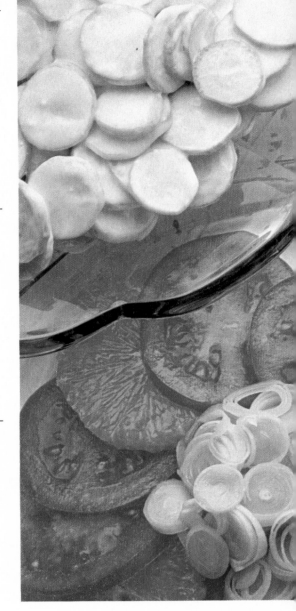

LEEK, TOMATO & ORANGE SALAD

Preparation time: 15 minutes
KJ/calorie count: 310/75, plus
    dressing

4 tomatoes, sliced
2 oranges, peeled and sliced
4 small leeks, finely sliced, using
    the white part only
lemon juice
Lemon Vinaigrette (page 57), to
    serve

1. Arrange the tomato and orange slices round the edge of a serving dish.
2. Put the leeks in the centre of the dish. Sprinkle the leeks with lemon juice. Serve with a Lemon Vinaigrette.

THREE BEAN SALAD

Preparation time: 10 minutes
KJ/calorie count: 585/140, plus
    dressing

225 g/8 oz cooked chick peas
225 g/8 oz cooked red kidney
    beans
225 g/8 oz cooked green beans
2 teaspoons chopped fresh mixed
    herbs or 1 teaspoon dried mixed
    herbs
Lemon Vinaigrette (page 57), to
    serve

1. Mix the chick peas and red kidney beans together in a salad bowl.
2. Cut the green beans into short pieces and add to the bean mixture.
3. Sprinkle with the herbs. Serve with a Lemon Vinaigrette.

CRUNCHY SALAD

Preparation time: 15 minutes
KJ/calorie count: 270/60, plus
    dressing

225 g/8 oz green pepper, cored,
    seeded and chopped
225 g/8 oz fennel, finely chopped
225 g/8 oz celery, roughly chopped
1 cucumber, peeled and diced
100 g/4 oz spring onions, chopped
1-2 teaspoons chopped fresh
    tarragon
Lemon Vinaigrette (page 57), to
    serve

1. Blanch the green pepper in boiling water for 1 minute. Drain.
2. Mix the pepper, fennel, celery, cucumber and spring onions together in a salad bowl and sprinkle with the tarragon. Serve with a Lemon Vinaigrette.

Right: Crunchy salad

MUSHROOM, COURGETTE & TOMATO SALAD

Preparation time: 15 minutes
KJ/calorie count: 190/45, plus dressing

6 large mushrooms, sliced
4 courgettes, peeled and thinly sliced
4 tomatoes, skinned and quartered
1 teaspoon chopped fresh basil
1 bunch watercress
Lemon Vinaigrette (page 57), to serve

1. Mix the mushrooms, courgettes and tomatoes together. Sprinkle with the basil.
2. Arrange the watercress in a serving dish and put the courgette mixture in the centre. Serve with a Lemon Vinaigrette.

Top left: Courgettes and yogurt
Top right: Three bean salad
Bottom left: Leek, tomato and orange salad
Bottom right: Mushroom, courgette and tomato salad

SMOKED MACKEREL SALAD

Preparation time: 15 minutes, plus draining
KJ/calorie count: 1210/290, plus dressing

1 cucumber, thinly sliced
salt
1 head of chicory
lettuce leaves
4 hard-boiled eggs, sliced
350 g/12 oz smoked mackerel, flaked
1 garlic clove, peeled and crushed
Lemon Vinaigrette (page 57), to serve

1. Place the cucumber on a plate, sprinkle with salt and cover with a second plate. Press down with a weight and leave for 30 minutes.
2. Arrange the chicory and lettuce leaves in a shallow bowl. Place the cucumber slices round the edge.
3. Arrange the egg slices next to the cucumber and arrange the flaked mackerel in the centre.
4. Stir the garlic into the Lemon Vinaigrette, and serve with the salad.

NORWEGIAN MACKEREL SALAD

Preparation time: 15 minutes
Cooking time: 15 minutes
KJ/calorie count: 1250/300

4 × 75 g/3 oz mackerel fillets
4 × 100 g/4 oz boiled potatoes, sliced
lettuce leaves
4 tomatoes, sliced

MUSTARD SAUCE:
4 tablespoons low-calorie mayonnaise
4 teaspoons French or English made mustard
salt
freshly ground black pepper

1. Place the mackerel under a preheated hot grill and cook for about 15 minutes, turning occasionally. Leave to cool, then remove the skin with a sharp knife.
2. Divide the flesh into pieces and arrange on 4 plates.
3. Place the potato slices on one side of the plates. On the other side, place the lettuce leaves and tomato slices.
4. Mix the mayonnaise, mustard, salt and pepper together. Serve the sauce separately or pour over the mackerel.

SEAFOOD & ASPARAGUS

Preparation time: 15 minutes
Cooking time: about 15 minutes
KJ/calorie count: 585/140

225 g/8 oz cod
8 fresh asparagus stalks, or 1 × 225 g/8 oz can asparagus spears, drained
lettuce leaves
100 g/4 oz peeled prawns
1 × 100 g/4 oz can mussels, drained
chopped fresh dill, to garnish
plain unsweetened yogurt, to serve
salt
freshly ground black pepper

1. Poach the cod in the minimum of water for 10-15 minutes. Drain, cool and flake with a fork.
2. Meanwhile cook the fresh asparagus, if using.
3. Line a salad bowl with lettuce leaves and arrange the prawns, mussels and asparagus around the edge.
4. Place the cod in the centre and sprinkle with dill. If liked, serve with plain unsweetened yogurt with a little dill, salt and pepper stirred in.

Top left: Prawn and rice salad
Top right: Smoked mackerel salad
Bottom left: Seafood and asparagus
Bottom right: Norwegian mackerel salad

PRAWN & RICE SALAD

Preparation time: 10 minutes, plus cooling
Cooking time: about 12 minutes
KJ/calorie count: 1020/245

100 g/4 oz long-grain rice
Fish Stock (page 16) (optional)
lettuce leaves
1 cucumber, peeled and sliced
4 tomatoes, skinned and quartered
450 g/1 lb peeled prawns
grated rind and juice of 1 lemon
pinch of paprika or cayenne

1. Cook the rice in a saucepan of boiling fish stock, or salted water, for about 12 minutes until just tender. Drain and leave to cool.
2. Place the lettuce in a salad bowl and add the cucumber slices and quartered tomatoes.
3. Mix the prawns and cold rice together. Stir in the lemon rind and paprika or cayenne.
4. Spoon into the centre of the bowl and sprinkle over the lemon juice.

VARIATIONS:
For a hotter flavoured salad, use tabasco sauce instead of the paprika or cayenne and lemon juice. Add 50 g/2 oz cooked peas to the salad.
KJ/calorie count: 1130/270

ITALIAN SALAD

Preparation time: 15 minutes
KJ/calorie count: 703/175 – turkey and veal; 1045/250 – chicken, plus dressing

350 g/12 oz cooked chicken, turkey or veal
8 tomatoes
1 fennel bulb, trimmed and roughly chopped
lettuce leaves
1 × 50 g/2 oz can anchovies, drained and rinsed
Lemon Vinaigrette (page 57), to serve

1. Cut the poultry or veal into bite-sized pieces.
2. Roughly chop 4 of the tomatoes and mix with the fennel.
3. Arrange the lettuce on a large platter. Slice the remaining tomatoes and place in a ring on top of the lettuce.
4. Mix the meat with the tomato and fennel mixture and spoon into the centre of the tomato ring.
5. Place the anchovies in a criss-cross pattern on top of the salad. Serve with a Lemon Vinaigrette.

PASTA SALAD

Preparation time: 15 minutes, plus cooling
Cooking time: 10 minutes
KJ/calorie count: 1045/250, plus dressing

100 g/4 oz shell or small shapes of pasta
about 300 ml/½ pint chicken stock
4 sticks celery, halved lengthwise and cut into strips
1 small red pepper, cored, seeded and cut into strips
4 large tomatoes, quartered
1 garlic clove, peeled and crushed
1 tablespoon chopped fresh basil
100 g/4 oz Mozzarella cheese, grated
Lemon Vinaigrette (page 57), to serve

1. Cook the pasta in the boiling stock for about 10 minutes until just tender. Drain and leave to cool.
2. Mix the celery, pepper, tomatoes, garlic, pasta and basil together.
3. Sprinkle with the grated cheese. Serve with a Lemon Vinaigrette.

Top: Italian salad
Left: Egg and cheese salad bowl
Right: Pasta salad

EGG & CHEESE SALAD BOWL

Preparation time: 15 minutes
KJ/calorie count: 1045/250, plus dressing

4 hard-boiled eggs, quartered
1 green pepper, cored, seeded and chopped
100 g/4 oz Edam cheese, cubed
4 sticks celery, roughly chopped
100 g/4 oz raisins
lettuce leaves
2 eating apples, preferably Cox's Orange Pippins or Granny Smith, cored, sliced and dipped in lemon juice
low-calorie mayonnaise, to serve

1. Gently mix the eggs, pepper, cheese, celery and raisins together.
2. Line a salad bowl with lettuce leaves and spoon in the egg mixture. Arrange the apple slices on top. Serve with low-calorie mayonnaise.

SPINACH, AVOCADO & WALNUT SALAD

Preparation time: 15 minutes
Cooking time: 5 minutes
KJ/calorie count: 840/200, plus
  dressing

450 g/1 lb young spinach, trimmed
100 g/4 oz lean ham, cut into strips
1 small avocado pear, peeled,
  stoned and sliced
50 g/2 oz walnuts
1 small orange, peeled and sliced
Orange Vinaigrette (page 57), to
  serve

1. Roughly tear the spinach leaves and place in a salad bowl.
2. Add the ham, avocado and walnuts.
3. Arrange the orange slices on top. Serve with an Orange Vinaigrette.

**Left: Spinach, avocado
and walnut salad**

SALAD DRESSINGS

CURRY VINAIGRETTE

Preparation time: 5 minutes
KJ/calorie count: 2 teaspoons – 145/35

4 tablespoons malt vinegar
4 tablespoons sunflower oil
2 teaspoons salt
2 teaspoons curry paste

This dressing is very good with prawns and other fish.

1. Place all the ingredients in a bowl and stir to mix thoroughly.
2. Alternatively, shake together in a screw-topped jar.

LEMON VINAIGRETTE

Preparation time: 5 minutes
*KJ/calorie count: 2 teaspoons –
145/35*

150 ml/¼ pint olive oil
1 tablespoon wine vinegar
2 tablespoons lemon juice
grated rind of 1 lemon
1 teaspoon French mustard
salt
freshly ground black pepper

1. Place all the ingredients in a bowl and stir to mix thoroughly.
2. Alternatively, shake together in a screw-topped jar.

VARIATION:
Orange juice can be used instead of lemon juice, omitting the rind.

YOGURT & LEMON DRESSING

*Preparation time: 5 minutes, plus
chilling*
*KJ/calorie count: half quantity –
145/35*

150 ml/¼ pint plain unsweetened
yogurt
1 tablespoon lemon juice
2 teaspoons chopped fresh herbs:
use mint for cucumber salad,
basil for tomato salad, and
fennel for green salad
salt
freshly ground black pepper

1. Mix the yogurt, lemon juice, appropriate herb, salt and pepper together in a bowl.
2. Chill for 1 hour before serving.

SPICY TOMATO SAUCE

Preparation time: 5 minutes
Cooking time: 1 hour
*KJ/calorie count: half quantity –
225/54*

250 ml/8 fl oz tomato juice
250 ml/8 fl oz wine vinegar
1 teaspoon Worcestershire sauce
50 g/2 oz finely chopped onion
2 teaspoons chopped fresh basil or
1 teaspoon dried basil
salt
freshly ground black pepper
artificial liquid sweetener, to taste

Serve this sauce hot with spaghetti, fish or plain grilled meat such as liver.

1. Put all the ingredients into a saucepan and bring to the boil.
2. Cover and simmer for 1 hour or until the sauce is thick enough for your taste. Taste and adjust the seasoning.
3. If stored in a screw-topped bottle in the refrigerator, this sauce will keep for up to 1 week.

VARIATION:
Add 2 teaspoons grated horseradish to the cooked sauce. This makes a very good sauce to serve with cold chicken or turkey.

HOT CURRY SAUCE

Preparation time: 5 minutes
Cooking time: about 15 minutes
KJ/calorie count: 40/10

1 medium marrow, peeled, sliced
and seeded
salt
about 2 teaspoons curry paste

This sauce is very good served with hard-boiled eggs or fish.

1. Cook the marrow in boiling salted water for 10-15 minutes until tender. Drain and cool.
2. Put 225 g/8 oz cooked marrow and the curry paste into a blender and liquidize until smooth.
3. Pour the mixture into a saucepan and reheat thoroughly.

Top left: Curry vinaigrette
Bottom left: Hot curry sauce
Centre: Spicy tomato sauce
Top right: Lemon vinaigrette
**Bottom right: Yogurt and
lemon dressing**

FISH

ORANGE HALIBUT

Preparation time: 5 minutes
Cooking time: 20 minutes
KJ/calorie count: about 500/120

4 × 100 g/4 oz halibut steaks
250 ml/8 fl oz unsweetened orange
   juice
2 teaspoons cornflour
1 teaspoon grated orange rind
1 tablespoon water
salt
freshly ground black pepper

1. Put the halibut steaks in a wide shallow pan and add the orange juice. Simmer for about 15 minutes until the fish is tender.
2. Place the fish on a heated serving dish and keep warm.
3. Blend the cornflour and orange rind with the water and add to the orange juice. Cook for 3 minutes. Add a little more orange juice if the sauce is too thick, and season with salt and pepper to taste.
4. Pour the orange sauce over the halibut or serve separately.

VARIATION:
Instead of orange juice use the same quantity of unsweetened pineapple juice.

SOLE FLORENTINE

Preparation time: 5 minutes
Cooking time: 20 minutes
*KJ/calorie count: 1500/360 (according
   to size of sole)*

4 Dover sole
lemon juice
50 g/2 oz butter
750 g/1½ lb cooked spinach,
   chopped or 2 × 275 g/10 oz
   packets frozen spinach, thawed
   and drained
300 ml/½ pint plain unsweetened
   yogurt
salt
freshly ground black pepper

For a more economical meal, lemon sole may be used in place of the Dover sole.

1. Sprinkle the fish with lemon juice and dot with half the butter.
2. Place under a preheated hot grill for about 15 minutes, turning frequently and using more lemon juice and the remaining butter to prevent burning.
3. Put the chopped spinach in a saucepan with the yogurt and heat gently, stirring continuously. Do not boil as the yogurt will curdle. Add salt and pepper to taste.
4. Place the spinach mixture on a large heated serving dish and arrange the grilled fish on top.

Top: Orange halibut
Bottom: Sole florentine

PORTUGUESE FISH

Preparation time: 10 minutes
Cooking time: 1 hour
KJ/calorie count: 420/100

4 × 100 g/4 oz pieces white fish,
   e.g. cod, coley, halibut

SAUCE:
8 tomatoes, skinned and chopped
1 onion, peeled and finely
   chopped
½ garlic clove, peeled and crushed
1 bay leaf
salt
freshly ground black pepper
1 tablespoon tomato juice
1 tablespoon wine vinegar

1. To make the sauce, put all the sauce ingredients in a heavy-based saucepan and simmer for 1 hour, uncovered. If the liquid reduces too quickly, add a little more tomato juice.
2. Meanwhile, place the fish in a wide shallow pan, and poach it in the minimum of water for about 15 minutes until tender.
3. Arrange the fish pieces on a heated serving dish and spoon the sauce over.

SEAFOOD COCKTAIL SALAD

Preparation time: 15 minutes
Cooking time: 4-5 minutes
KJ/calorie count: 920/220

4 scallops, prepared
100 g/4 oz white fish
100 g/4 oz peeled prawns
shredded lettuce leaves
8 tomatoes, skinned and
   quartered

SAUCE:
120 ml/4 fl oz low-calorie
   mayonnaise
1 dessertspoon tomato purée
1 teaspoon chopped fresh basil or
   ½ teaspoon dried basil
salt
freshly ground black pepper

1. Place the scallops and white fish in a saucepan. Poach in the minimum of water for about 4-5 minutes until tender. Drain and cool.
2. Flake the fish using a fork. Cut the scallops into small pieces. Add the prawns to the fish mixture.
3. Mix the low-calorie mayonnaise, tomato purée, basil, salt and pepper together, then stir into the fish.
4. Place the shredded lettuce on a serving dish and surround with the tomato quarters.
5. Spoon the fish mixture into the centre of the dish.

DEVILLED FISH

Preparation time: 2 minutes
Cooking time: about 20 minutes
KJ/calorie count: about 380/90

4 × 100 g/4 oz pieces coley or cod
120 ml/4 fl oz lemon juice
2 teaspoons Worcestershire sauce
1 teaspoon French mustard
salt
freshly ground black pepper
artificial liquid sweetener, to taste

1. Place the fish in a casserole dish.
2. Mix together the remaining ingredients and pour them over the fish.
3. Cover and cook in a preheated oven at 190°C, 375°F, Gas Mark 5 for about 20 minutes or until the fish is tender.

VARIATION:
Marinate the fish in the lemon juice, Worcestershire sauce and mustard for 2 hours. Cook under a preheated medium grill for about 15 minutes using the marinade for basting. Turn frequently.

Top left: Portuguese fish
Bottom left: Seafood
cocktail salad
Top right: Cold curried prawns
Bottom right: Devilled fish

COLD CURRIED PRAWNS

Preparation time: 5 minutes, plus marinating
KJ/calorie count: 920/220

450 g/1 lb peeled prawns

SAUCE:
4 tablespoons sunflower oil
4 teaspoons curry paste
8 tablespoons wine vinegar
pinch of salt

1. Put the prawns in a shallow dish.
2. Mix the sunflower oil, curry paste and wine vinegar together. Add a pinch of salt, unless the prawns are already salty.
3. Pour the sauce over the prawns and leave to marinate for 1 hour in a cool place, turning frequently. Serve the prawns in the sauce.

KIPPER SOUFFLÉ

Preparation time: 20 minutes
Cooking time: 30 minutes
KJ/calorie count: 1360/325

350 g/12 oz kippers
25 g/1 oz butter
25 g/1 oz plain flour
300 ml/½ pint skimmed milk
salt
freshly ground black pepper
2 eggs, separated

1. Place the kippers in a wide saucepan. Cook in the minimum of water for about 10 minutes until soft. Alternatively, place in a deep jug and cover with boiling water. Leave for 5-10 minutes, then drain.
2. Mash the kippers. Melt the butter in a saucepan and stir in the flour. Cook for 2 minutes, stirring. Remove from the heat.
3. Gradually add the skimmed milk, stirring well after each addition.
4. Return to the heat and mix in the

mashed kipper. Add salt, if necessary, and plenty of pepper.
5. Remove from the heat and stir the egg yolks into the mixture. Whisk the egg whites until they will form stiff peaks and fold in.
6. Turn into a lightly buttered soufflé dish and bake in a preheated oven at 200°C, 400°F, Gas Mark 6 for 20 minutes if you like a runny centre or 25 minutes for a drier soufflé.

MACKEREL FISH CAKES

Preparation time: 20 minutes
Cooking time: 10 minutes
KJ/calorie count: 1110/265

350 g/12 oz cooked or canned
  mackerel
350 g/12 oz cooked potatoes
1 tablespoon curry powder
salt
freshly ground black pepper
oil

1. If using canned mackerel, drain well. Mash the fish and potatoes together using a fork and potato masher. Mix in the curry powder and salt and pepper to taste.
2. Cover the grill rack with foil and brush or spray with oil.
3. Shape the mixture into 12 fish cakes and place under a hot grill. Cook for about 5 minutes on each side until browned.

VARIATIONS:
Use 2 teaspoons chopped fresh sage or 1 teaspoon dried sage instead of curry powder.
Use cooked or canned salmon and 2 teaspoons chopped fresh tarragon or 1 teaspoon dried tarragon instead of mackerel and curry powder.

SMOKED HADDOCK KEDGEREE

Preparation time: 5 minutes
Cooking time: about 20 minutes
KJ/calorie count: 1090/260

350 g/12 oz smoked haddock
75 g/3 oz long grain rice
salt
225 g/8 oz peas
1 tablespoon chopped onion
2 hard-boiled eggs, chopped
1 teaspoon curry paste
salt
freshly ground black pepper
chopped fresh parsley, to garnish

1. Place the haddock in a saucepan. Poach in the minimum of water for about 12 minutes until tender, then drain and flake into small pieces using a fork.
2. Meanwhile, cook the rice in boiling salted water for about 12 minutes, then drain.
3. Cook the peas and chopped onion in boiling salted water for about 6 minutes, then drain.
4. Mix the fish, rice, peas, onion, chopped hard-boiled eggs and curry paste together and add salt and pepper to taste. Serve garnished with chopped fresh parsley.

VARIATION:
Serve the kedgeree cold tossed in low-calorie mayonnaise.

TUNA-STUFFED GLOBE ARTICHOKES

Preparation time: 20 minutes
Cooking time: 30 minutes
KJ/calorie count: 1170/280

4 globe artichokes
salt
100 g/4 oz long grain rice
1 × 350 g/12 oz can tuna fish
4 tablespoons tomato purée
2 teaspoons chopped fresh basil or
  1 teaspoon dried basil
2 teaspoons chopped fresh
  oregano or 1 teaspoon dried
  oregano
salt
freshly ground black pepper

1. Cut off the artichoke stalks. Plunge the heads into boiling salted water. Simmer for about 20 minutes or until the bottom leaves pull away easily. Drain and leave until cold.
2. Remove the hairy chokes from the centre of the artichokes.
3. Meanwhile, cook the rice in boiling salted water for about 12 minutes. Drain and leave until cold.
4. Thoroughly drain the oil from the tuna fish and flake it using a fork. Add to the rice together with the tomato purée, herbs and salt and pepper to taste.
5. Fill each globe artichoke with the tuna and rice mixture. Serve with a tomato salad.

Top left: Kipper soufflé
Bottom left: Tuna-stuffed
globe artichokes

Top right: Mackerel fish cakes
Bottom right: Smoked
haddock kedgeree

PLUM FISH

Preparation time: 5 minutes
Cooking time: about 15 minutes
KJ/calorie count: 500/120

4 × 100 g/4 oz pieces cod, coley or
   halibut
lemon juice
salt
freshly ground black pepper

SAUCE:
450 g/1 lb ripe plums, peeled,
   halved and stoned
lemon juice
artificial liquid sweetener, to taste

1. Sprinkle the fish with lemon juice and salt and pepper. Cook under a preheated moderate grill for about 15 minutes, turning from time to time and sprinkling with more juice if necessary.
2. Meanwhile, make the sauce. Put the plums into a saucepan with enough lemon juice barely to cover and a little artificial sweetener.

3. Simmer gently for about 15 minutes until the plums are mushy. Taste and adjust the sweetness.
4. When the fish is cooked, arrange on a heated serving dish and pour the plum sauce over. Follow with a green salad.

ORANGE & PAPRIKA FISH

Preparation time: 5 minutes, plus
   marinating
Cooking time: 15 minutes
KJ/calorie count: 630/150

4 × 175 g/6 oz pieces skate or cod
250 ml/8 fl oz unsweetened orange
   juice
paprika
salt
freshly ground black pepper

This dish is particularly good served with a chicory and orange salad.

1. Place the fish in a shallow dish.
2. Mix the orange juice with 1 teaspoon paprika and salt and pepper and pour over the fish. Leave to marinate for 2 hours.
3. Drain the fish and place under a preheated hot grill for about 15 minutes, turning frequently and adding more paprika and orange juice marinade to prevent drying.

TROUT IN FOIL

Preparation time: 15 minutes
Cooking time: 30 minutes
KJ/calorie count: 1045/250 (according
   to size of trout)

1 carrot, peeled and finely
   chopped
few celery leaves, finely chopped
1 dessertspoon chopped fresh
   parsley
1 garlic clove, peeled and finely
   chopped
15 g/½ oz butter
4 small trout, cleaned
salt
freshly ground black pepper

1. Mix the carrot, celery leaves, parsley and garlic together. Melt the butter in a pan and fry the vegetables quickly for about 10 minutes until the mixture is soft.
2. Place each trout on a piece of foil large enough to cover the fish completely. Season with salt and pepper.
3. Divide the vegetable mixture into four and spoon it over the fish.
4. Wrap the fish in foil, tucking the ends in firmly. Bake in a preheated oven at 190°C, 375°F, Gas Mark 5 for about 20 minutes until tender. Serve the trout in the foil parcel.

Top left: Plum fish
Top right: Sole Veronica
Bottom left: Orange and
paprika fish
Bottom right: Trout in foil

SOLE VERONICA

Preparation time: 5 minutes
Cooking time: 20 minutes
KJ/calorie count: 840/200

4 × 100 g/4 oz pieces sole fillets
250 ml/8 fl oz grape juice
salt
freshly ground black pepper
40 grapes, deseeded

1. Put the sole in a wide shallow pan and pour over the grape juice. Season with salt and pepper.
2. Simmer for about 15 minutes until the fish is tender.
3. Add the grapes and cook for a further 5 minutes.
4. Place the fish on a heated serving dish and pour the sauce and grapes over.

MACKEREL IN A BAG

Preparation time: 5 minutes
Cooking time: 20 minutes
KJ/calorie count: 1210/290 (according to size of mackerel)

12 slices lemon
4 small mackerel, cleaned
2 teaspoons chopped fresh sage or
  1 teaspoon dried sage
salt
freshly ground black pepper
olive oil

1. Place 3 slices of lemon on each mackerel and sprinkle with the sage. Season with salt and pepper.
2. Lightly oil 4 pieces of greaseproof paper cut large enough to enclose the fish. Place the mackerel on the oiled paper and fold over to form a parcel.
3. Bake in a preheated oven at 190°C, 375°F, Gas Mark 5 for about 20 minutes or until the fish is tender. Serve the mackerel in the greaseproof bags.

SALMON BAKE

Preparation time: 5 minutes
Cooking time: 20 minutes
KJ/calorie count: 1170/280

350 g/12 oz cooked or canned
  salmon
2 eggs
350 ml/12 fl oz skimmed milk
50 g/2 oz Cheddar cheese, grated
salt
freshly ground black pepper

1. Flake the salmon with a fork, discarding the bones, and place in a casserole dish.
2. Beat together the eggs and milk, then stir in the cheese, salt and pepper.
3. Pour over the salmon and bake in a preheated oven at 180°C, 350°F, Gas Mark 4 for about 20 minutes or until the custard has set.

Above left: Salmon bake
Above right: Mackerel in a bag

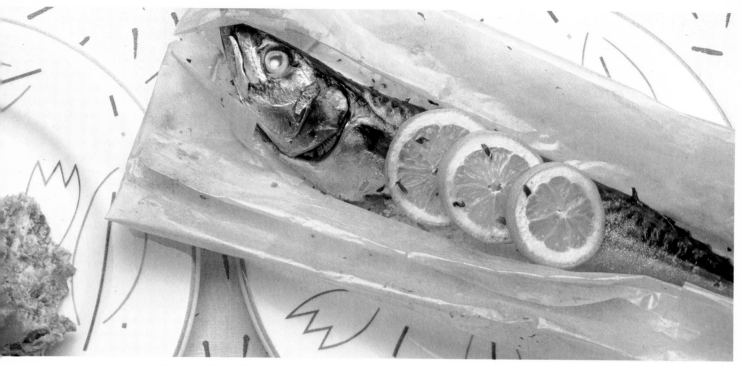

Below left: Fish and
tomato bake
Below right: Fish kebabs

FISH & TOMATO BAKE

Preparation time: 10 minutes
Cooking time: 25 minutes
KJ/calorie count: 1130/270

---

225 g/8 oz coley
100 g/4 oz cod
4 scallops, prepared
100 g/4 oz Cheddar or Gruyère
    cheese, grated
2 eggs
2 tablespoons dried skimmed milk
    powder
2 tablespoons water
salt
freshly ground black pepper
4 tomatoes, sliced

1. Place the white fish and scallops in a wide saucepan. Poach in water for about 4-5 minutes until tender. Drain.
2. Cut the scallops into quarters and the rest of the fish into chunks. Place in an ovenproof dish. Add most of the cheese, reserving some for the topping.
3. Beat the eggs and skimmed milk powder with the water. Add about 300 ml/½ pint of the fish cooking liquid and salt and pepper to taste, then pour it over the fish and cheese.
4. Arrange the sliced tomatoes on top of the dish. Sprinkle with the remaining cheese and bake in a preheated oven at 190°C, 375°F, Gas Mark 5 for about 20 minutes until the egg mixture has set.

FISH KEBABS

Preparation time: 10 minutes
Cooking time: 20 minutes
KJ/calorie count: 500/120

---

1 small green pepper, cored,
    seeded and roughly chopped
450 g/1 lb cod, cut into small cubes
4 firm tomatoes, quartered
12 grapes, seeded
8 button mushrooms, trimmed
8 bay leaves
lemon juice
2 teaspoons chopped fresh
    tarragon or 1 teaspoon dried

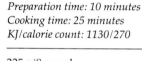

1. Place the chopped pepper in a saucepan and simmer in the minimum of water for 10 minutes. Drain.
2. Thread the fish cubes on to skewers with the tomato quarters, grapes, mushrooms, pieces of pepper and bay leaves.
3. Sprinkle the kebabs with lemon juice and tarragon. Place under a preheated moderate grill for about 10 minutes until the fish is cooked, turning frequently and sprinkling with more lemon juice if necessary.

COQUILLES ST JACQUES

Preparation time: 30 minutes
Cooking time: 20 minutes
KJ/calorie count: 1090/260

350 g/12 oz scallops, prepared
1 dessertspoon wine vinegar
350 g/12 oz potatoes, peeled
2 tablespoons dried skimmed milk
  powder
15 g/½ oz butter
1 dessertspoon plain flour
25 g/1 oz Gruyère cheese, grated

1. Gently poach the scallops in enough water to cover and the vinegar for 4-5 minutes until tender. Drain and reserve the poaching liquid.
2. Meanwhile, place the potatoes in a saucepan of salted water, bring to the boil and simmer for about 20 minutes until tender. Strain and reserve the cooking water.
3. Mash the potatoes with a little of the cooking water and ½ tablespoon of the skimmed milk powder.
4. Melt the butter in a saucepan and stir in the flour. Cook for 2 minutes, stirring.
5. Mix the remaining skimmed milk powder with the scallop poaching liquid and make up to about 300 ml/½ pint with the potato cooking water. Gradually add enough of this liquid to make a fairly thick sauce.
6. Put the drained scallops on their shells or in individual flameproof dishes.
7. Put the mashed potato into a piping bag fitted with a vegetable nozzle and pipe round the edge of the shells or dishes.
8. Pour on the sauce and sprinkle the cheese over. Place under a preheated hot grill until the cheese has melted and lightly browned.

HALIBUT WITH TARRAGON

Preparation time: 10 minutes, plus marinating
Cooking time: 15-20 minutes
KJ/calorie count: 540/130

4 × 175 g/6 oz halibut or cod steaks
grated rind and juice of 2-3 lemons
few sprigs of tarragon
salt
freshly ground black pepper

1. Place the halibut in a large shallow dish. Sprinkle over the lemon rind and juice, tarragon leaves, salt and pepper.
2. Turn the fish to coat with the lemon and herb mixture. Cover and leave to marinate for about 3 hours.
3. Place each piece of fish on a sheet of foil large enough to enclose it. Spoon over a little of the marinade and wrap up the fish.
4. Cook in a preheated oven at 200°C, 400°F, Gas Mark 6 for about 15-20 minutes, depending on the thickness of the halibut. Unwrap and serve on a heated dish.

HADDOCK CHARLOTTE

Preparation time: 10 minutes
Cooking time: 40-45 minutes
KJ/calorie count: 1045/250

450 g/1 lb haddock
175 g/6 oz canned sweetcorn, drained
1 large onion, peeled and chopped
50 g/2 oz button mushrooms, sliced
1 tablespoon chopped fresh parsley
300 ml/½ pint fish stock or water
salt
freshly ground black pepper
25 g/1 oz low-calorie spread
4 slices bread

1. Cut the haddock into small pieces and arrange in a casserole or soufflé dish.
2. Stir in the sweetcorn, onion, mushroom, parsley, stock or water, and salt and pepper to taste.
3. Spread a little low-calorie spread on to the bread slices, cut into quarters and arrange on top of the fish mixture.
4. Place in a preheated oven at 190°C, 375°F, Gas Mark 5 and bake for 40-45 minutes or until the fish is cooked and the bread topping browned.

NORWEGIAN BRAISED FISH

Preparation time: 20 minutes
Cooking time: about 30 minutes
KJ/calorie count: 1045/250

4 medium potatoes, peeled and thinly sliced
salt
25 g/1 oz chopped onion
1 green pepper, cored, seeded and cut into strips
4 tomatoes, skinned and sliced
4 × 175 g/6 oz cod steaks
2 tablespoons tomato purée
freshly ground black pepper

1. Place the potato slices in a saucepan of salted water. Bring to the boil, cover and simmer for about 10 minutes.
2. Drain, reserving the cooking water, and arrange on the base of a casserole dish. Sprinkle over the chopped onion.
3. Add the pepper and tomato slices to the dish. Place the cod steaks on top.
4. Mix the tomato purée and about 300 ml/½ pint potato cooking water together and pour over the fish; it should come about half way up the casserole dish. Add salt and pepper.
5. Cover and cook in a preheated oven at 200°C, 400°F, Gas Mark 6 for about 30 minutes until the fish is tender.

VARIATION:
Omit the potatoes. Sprinkle 75 g/3 oz grated Jarlsberg or Cheddar cheese on top of the cooked fish and place under a hot grill for a few minutes to brown.

Top left: Coquilles St Jacques
Top right: Halibut with tarragon
Below left: Haddock charlotte
Below right: Norwegian braised fish

POULTRY & GAME

SPRING CHICKEN WITH MUSHROOM STUFFING

Preparation time: 10-15 minutes
Cooking time: 40 minutes-1 hour
KJ/calorie count: 100 g/4 oz chicken meat without skin with 1 heaped dessertspoon stuffing: 1500/360

2 spring chickens or 4 poussins
butter

STUFFING:
225 g/8 oz mushrooms, chopped
100 g/4 oz onions, peeled and finely chopped
1 tablespoon tomato purée
50 g/2 oz fresh breadcrumbs
1 teaspoon chopped fresh parsley
salt
freshly ground black pepper
1 egg, beaten, to bind

1. Mix the stuffing ingredients together and bind together with the beaten egg. Spoon the stuffing into the body cavities of the chickens or poussins.
2. Place a knob of butter on each bird and wrap completely in foil.
3. Roast in a preheated oven at 200°C, 400°F, Gas Mark 6 until the chickens are tender, about 1 hour for the spring chickens or 40 minutes for the poussins.
4. Unfold the top of the foil 10 minutes before the end of the cooking time to allow the birds to brown.

POUSSINS WITH TARRAGON

Preparation time: 10 minutes
Cooking time: about 45 minutes (depending on size of bird)
KJ/calorie count: 1250/300

4 poussins
2 lemons
1 dessertspoon chopped fresh tarragon or 1 teaspoon dried tarragon
salt
freshly ground black pepper
4 knobs butter

1. Place the poussins on pieces of foil large enough to cover them.
2. Cut the lemons in half and squeeze a lemon half over each poussin. Cut the halves into quarters and put 2 quarters into the body cavity of each bird.
3. Sprinkle each poussin with the tarragon and salt and pepper. Place a knob of butter on each bird and wrap firmly in the foil.
4. Cook in a preheated oven at 180°C, 350°F, Gas Mark 4 for 25 minutes.
5. Open the foil and turn the birds over. After 5 minutes, turn the birds back, breast side up.
6. Leave the foil open and cook for a further 10 minutes to brown the poussins.
7. Transfer the poussins to a heated serving dish and pour the cooking liquid over them. They can be served hot or cold. When served cold the tarragon mixture turns to jelly.

Top: Spring chicken with mushroom stuffing
Bottom: Poussins with tarragon

SLIMMERS' COQ-AU-VIN

Preparation time: 20 minutes, plus
  marinating
Cooking time: about 1 hour
KJ/calorie count: 920/220

4 × 175 g/6 oz chicken portions
225 g/8 oz button onions, peeled
  or larger onions, peeled and
  sliced
900 ml/1½ pints chicken stock
225 g/8 oz button mushrooms
chopped fresh parsley, to garnish

MARINADE:
1 garlic clove, peeled and crushed
150 ml/¼ pint wine vinegar
150 ml/¼ pint red wine
1 tablespoon Worcestershire sauce
salt
freshly ground black pepper

1. Mix the marinade ingredients together.
2. Skin the chicken, place in a dish and pour the marinade over. Marinate for at least 3 hours in a cool place.
3. Remove the chicken portions from the marinade and cook under a preheated hot grill for about 10 minutes, turning frequently.
4. Transfer the chicken to a casserole with the onions and stock. Cover and cook in a preheated oven at 220°C, 425°F, Gas Mark 7 for about 50 minutes.
5. Add the mushrooms and cook for a further 10 minutes or until the chicken portions are tender. To test, pierce the chicken with a sharp knife, if the juices run clear the chicken is cooked.
6. Meanwhile, pour the marinade into a saucepan and boil for 5 minutes. Pour over the casserole and garnish with the parsley.

WEST INDIAN CHICKEN

Preparation time: 10 minutes, plus
  marinating
Cooking time: 35 minutes
KJ/calorie count: 1170/280

4 × 175 g/6 oz chicken portions
1 teaspoon curry powder, or to
  taste
1 teaspoon ground ginger
1 × 225 g/8 oz can pineapple
  chunks
1 green pepper, cored, seeded and
  chopped
salt
freshly ground black pepper

1. Skin the chicken portions and score the flesh with a sharp knife.
2. Mix the curry powder and ginger together and rub into the chicken flesh.
3. Place the chicken in a shallow dish and pour over the pineapple juice from the can. Marinate for 2 hours.
4. Put the chicken under a hot grill and cook for about 20 minutes until tender, turning frequently and using the marinade to baste and prevent burning.
5. Put the pineapple chunks, remaining marinade and chopped pepper into a blender and liquidize until smooth.
6. Pour the purée into a pan and heat through. Taste and adjust the seasoning.
7. Place the grilled chicken joints on a heated serving dish and pour the sauce over or serve it separately. Serve with a green salad.

BRAISED SPRING CHICKEN

Preparation time: 10 minutes
Cooking time: about 1 hour
KJ/calorie count: 1250/300

4-6 large flat mushrooms
2 teaspoons chopped fresh thyme
  or 1 teaspoon dried thyme
4 slices lean ham, without fat
2 spring chickens, prepared
salt
freshly ground black pepper
1 wine glass white wine

1. Cut off the mushroom stalks and place the mushrooms in the bottom of a large casserole. Sprinkle over the thyme. Lay the slices of ham over the mushrooms.
2. Place the spring chickens on top. Add salt, pepper and the white wine.
3. Cover and cook in a preheated oven at 200°C, 400°F, Gas Mark 6 for about 1 hour. Uncover and continue cooking for 5 minutes.
4. Cut each spring chicken in half and serve on a bed of mushrooms and ham.

Far left: Slimmers' coq-au-vin
Top and right: Braised spring chicken
Below: Chicken from Provence

CHICKEN FROM PROVENCE

Preparation time: 10 minutes
Cooking time: about 25 minutes
KJ/calorie count: 880/210

1 garlic clove, peeled and crushed
4 × 175 g/6 oz chicken portions, skinned
lemon juice

SAUCE:
100 g/4 oz button mushrooms
25 g/1 oz chopped onion
120 ml/4 fl oz unsweetened apple juice
120 ml/4 fl oz wine vinegar
120 ml/4 fl oz tomato juice
salt
freshly ground black pepper
1 teaspoon cornflour (optional)

1. Rub the crushed garlic over the chicken flesh.
2. Put the chicken under a preheated hot grill and cook for about 25 minutes, turning frequently and using the lemon juice for basting.
3. Meanwhile, put all the sauce ingredients in a saucepan, except the cornflour, and simmer, uncovered, for 25 minutes. Add salt and pepper to taste.
4. For a thicker sauce, mix the cornflour with 2 teaspoons cold water. Stir into the sauce and simmer for another 3 minutes.
5. Place the chicken portions on a heated serving dish, pour the sauce over and serve.

CARIBBEAN CHICKEN

Preparation time: 10 minutes
Cooking time: 1 hour
KJ/calorie count: 1190/285

4 × 175 g/6 oz chicken portions
1 large red pepper, cored, seeded and chopped
1 teaspoon curry powder
250 ml/8 fl oz chicken stock
salt
freshly ground black pepper
4 fresh or canned pineapple rings
1 banana
1 orange, peeled and sliced, to garnish

1. Put the chicken portions in a casserole with the chopped pepper and curry powder. Pour over the stock and add salt and pepper.
2. Cover and cook in a preheated oven at 220°C, 425°F, Gas Mark 7 for 50 minutes.
3. Chop the pineapple rings and banana and add to the casserole. Cook for a further 10 minutes or until the chicken is tender.
4. Garnish the casserole with the orange slices.

Left: West Indian chicken
Right: Caribbean chicken

CHICKEN WITH PRUNE & APPLE STUFFING

Preparation time: 15 minutes
Cooking time: about 1½ hours
KJ/calorie count: 75 g/3 oz chicken meat without skin with 1 heaped dessertspoon stuffing: 1570/375

1 × 1.5 kg/3 lb chicken

STUFFING:
175 g/6 oz fresh breadcrumbs
12 prunes, soaked overnight and chopped
2 large apples, cored and cut into chunks
grated rind and juice of 1 lemon
1 egg, beaten
skimmed milk, if necessary
salt
freshly ground black pepper

1. For the stuffing, mix together the breadcrumbs, prunes, apple and lemon rind. Add the beaten egg and lemon juice to bind. If necessary, stir in a little milk. Add salt and pepper to taste.
2. Spoon the stuffing into the body cavity of the bird.
3. Place the chicken into a roasting tin half filled with water and roast for about 1½ hours in a preheated oven at 200°C, 400°F, Gas Mark 6. Baste frequently.

VARIATION:
Stuff the chicken with 4 tablespoons sweetcorn kernels, 1 tablespoon chopped onion, 1 tablespoon chopped fresh parsley, salt and freshly ground black pepper mixed together.
KJ/calorie count: 75 g/3 oz chicken meat without skin with 1 heaped dessertspoon stuffing: 872/217

CITRUS CHICKEN

Preparation time: 5 minutes
Cooking time: about 2½ hours
*KJ/calorie count: 75 g/3 oz chicken
    meat without skin with sauce:
    1130/270*

1 × 1.5 kg/3 lb chicken
2 small turnips, peeled
2 carrots, peeled
grated rind of 1 lemon
100 g/4 oz onion, peeled and
    chopped
salt
freshly ground black pepper
2 tablespoons lemon juice
1 large wine glass wine vinegar
artificial liquid sweetener
    (optional)
1 tablespoon cornflour
orange slices, to garnish

1. Place the chicken in a large saucepan with the turnips, carrots, lemon rind, chopped onion, salt and pepper.
2. Cover with water and bring to the boil. Cover and simmer for about 2 hours, skimming the water occasionally.
3. When the bird is cooked, remove from the pan. Spoon 300 ml/½ pint stock into a saucepan with the lemon juice, wine vinegar and artificial sweetener, if used. Simmer for 4 minutes.
4. Blend the cornflour with a little of the remaining stock. Add to the mixture and cook for 3 minutes until fairly thick and almost transparent.
5. Carve the chicken into slices and place on a heated serving dish. Pour over the lemon and vinegar sauce and leave to cool. Garnish with the orange slices.
6. If liked, serve with the vegetables cooked with the chicken or with a green salad.

BOILED CHICKEN WITH TARRAGON RICE

Preparation time: 10 minutes
*Cooking time: 2 hours (depending on
    age of bird)*
*KJ/calorie count: 100 g/4 oz chicken
    meat with 75 g/3 oz tarragon rice:
    1250/300*

1 × 1.5 kg/3 lb boiling fowl
1 large carrot, peeled
1 small turnip, peeled
1 large onion, peeled
1 bouquet garni
salt
freshly ground black pepper
TARRAGON RICE:
100 g/4 oz long-grain rice
salt
1 red pepper, cored seeded and
    sliced
1 tablespoon tarragon vinegar
1 tablespoon olive oil
freshly ground black pepper
1 dessertspoon chopped fresh
    tarragon or 1 teaspoon dried
    tarragon

1. Put the boiling fowl in a large saucepan with the whole carrot, turnip and onion. Add the bouquet garni, salt and pepper. Cover with water and bring to the boil. Cover and simmer for about 2 hours (depending on the age of the bird), skimming the water occasionally.
2. Put the rice in a saucepan of boiling salted water and simmer for 12-15 minutes or until cooked but still slightly firm.
3. Blanch the pepper in boiling water for 1 minute. Drain the rice and add the red pepper.
4. Stir in the tarragon vinegar, olive oil and salt and pepper to taste. Spoon into a heated serving dish and sprinkle with the chopped tarragon.
5. Remove the bird from the pan, take off the skin and carve the meat.
6. Serve the chicken with the tarragon rice. Also delicious served cold.

**Top: Chicken with prune and
apple stuffing
Below left: Boiled chicken with
tarragon rice
Below right: Citrus chicken**

ROAST PHEASANT

Preparation time: 10 minutes
Cooking time: about 2 hours
KJ/calorie count: 750/180 per 75 g/
    3 oz portion

oil
1 large pheasant, prepared
salt
freshly ground black pepper

1. Smear a piece of kitchen foil, large enough to enclose the pheasant, all over with a little oil.
2. Season the pheasant with salt and pepper, then wrap in the foil. Place the bird on its side on a rack in a roasting tin.
3. Roast in a preheated oven at 200°C, 400°F, Gas Mark 6 for about 2 hours or until tender, turning the pheasant over every 30 minutes. (Cooking time depends on the age of the bird.)
4. Remove the pheasant from the foil and serve hot with Bread Sauce (see below) and baked potatoes or allow to cool and serve cold with an orange and chicory salad.

BREAD SAUCE

Preparation time: 5 minutes
Cooking time: about 8 minutes
KJ/calorie count: 420/100

1 dessertspoon chopped onion
450 ml/¾ pint skimmed milk
100 g/4 oz white breadcrumbs
2-3 bay leaves
¼ teaspoon ground coriander
salt
freshly ground black pepper

1. Simmer the onion in a little of the skimmed milk until soft.
2. Add the breadcrumbs, bay leaves, coriander and salt and pepper with the rest of the milk.
3. Stir thoroughly and simmer for a further 5 minutes, stirring constantly.
4. Remove the bay leaves and serve immediately.

Roast pheasant with bread sauce

CHICKEN & VEGETABLE CASSEROLE

Preparation time: 15 minutes
Cooking time: about 1½ hours
KJ/calorie count: 1380/330

1 medium onion, peeled and
  roughly chopped
3-4 celery sticks, roughly chopped
4 carrots, peeled and roughly
  chopped
4 turnips, peeled and roughly
  chopped
1 small swede, peeled and roughly
  chopped
4 × 225 g/8 oz chicken joints,
  skinned
1 bay leaf
1 bouquet garni
300 ml/½ pint chicken stock
salt
freshly ground black pepper

1. Place half of the vegetables in a casserole. Put the chicken joints on top and cover with the remaining vegetables.
2. Add the bay leaf, bouquet garni, stock, salt and pepper. If using a flameproof casserole, bring to the boil on top of the cooker and skim.
3. Cover and cook in a preheated oven at 180°C, 350°F, Gas Mark 4 for about 1½ hours.
4. Skim off any fat and serve. Alternatively, leave overnight and remove the fat, then reheat in the oven for about 30 minutes.

MUSHROOM CHICKEN CASSEROLE

Preparation time: 10 minutes
Cooking time: 35-40 minutes
KJ/calorie count: 840/200

4 × 175 g/6 oz chicken joints
175 g/6 oz mushrooms
25 g/1 oz chopped onion
250 ml/8 fl oz chicken stock
salt
freshly ground black pepper

1. Skin the chicken and place in a casserole with the mushrooms, whole if small or sliced if large.
2. Add the chopped onion, stock and salt and pepper. Cover and cook in a preheated oven at 220°C, 425°F, Gas Mark 7 for 35-40 minutes or until the chicken is tender, when pierced with a sharp knife the juices run clear. Serve immediately.

CHICKEN TANDOORI

Preparation time: 15 minutes, plus marinating
Cooking time: 20 minutes
KJ/calorie count: 1045/250

4 × 175 g/6 oz chicken breasts,
  skinned
1 garlic clove, peeled and crushed
1 tablespoon tandoori powder
300 ml/½ pint plain unsweetened
  yogurt

1. Make incisions in the chicken flesh with a sharp knife. Rub in the garlic. Mix the tandoori powder with the yogurt and rub some of this mixture well into the incisions.
2. Pour the remaining mixture over the joints and leave to marinate for about 4 hours, turning occasionally.
3. Remove the chicken from the marinade and place under a preheated medium grill. Cook for about 20 minutes, turning frequently and spooning over the marinade a little at a time, to prevent burning. All the marinade should be used to thinly coat the chicken.

Far left: Chicken and vegetable casserole
Centre: Mushroom chicken casserole
Right: Chicken tandoori

CHICKEN WITH PEPPERS

Preparation time: 15 minutes
KJ/calorie count: 840/200

---

350 g/12 oz cooked chicken meat

1 large green pepper, cored, seeded and sliced

1 large red pepper, cored, seeded and sliced

1 medium avocado, peeled, stoned and chopped

2 tablespoons low-calorie mayonnaise

1. Cut the chicken meat into bite-sized pieces.
2. Blanch the peppers in boiling water for 1 minute.
3. Mix the pepper, avocado and chicken together then stir in the low-calorie mayonnaise. Serve with a green salad.

CHICKEN RISOTTO

Preparation time: 5 minutes
Cooking time: 20 minutes
KJ/calorie count: served hot: 1045/250
served cold: 1360/325

---

100 g/4 oz long-grain rice

500 ml/18 fl oz chicken stock

350 g/12 oz cooked chicken meat

1 dessertspoon chopped fresh tarragon or 1 teaspoon dried tarragon

salt

freshly ground black pepper

1. Put the rice in a saucepan and cover with the stock, reserving a little. Cover the pan and cook briskly, adding more stock if necessary.
2. Cut the chicken into bite-sized pieces.
3. Remove the rice from the heat when nearly cooked, after about 12 minutes. Stir in the tarragon and chicken.
4. Add more stock if the mixture is too dry and return to the heat for about 5 minutes until the chicken is hot. Add salt and pepper to taste. All the stock should be absorbed, if not, drain. Serve immediately.

VARIATION:
This dish is also very good cold. Make as above and then leave to cool thoroughly. Mix in 1 tablespoon tarragon vinegar and 1 tablespoon olive oil.

HERBED CHICKEN PASTA

Preparation time: 5 minutes
Cooking time: 20 minutes
KJ/calorie count: 1250/300

---

100 g/4 oz shell pasta or macaroni

1 teaspoon chopped fresh oregano or ½ teaspoon dried oregano

1 teaspoon chopped fresh rosemary or ½ teaspoon dried rosemary

350 g/12 oz cooked chicken meat

100 g/4 oz mushrooms, chopped

1 tablespoon olive oil

1 teaspoon ground coriander

salt

freshly ground black pepper

1. Put the pasta into boiling, salted water with the herbs and cook for about 10 minutes until tender but still firm.
2. Cut the chicken meat into bite-sized pieces.
3. Add the chicken and mushrooms to the pasta and cook for a further 10 minutes. Drain if necessary.
4. Add the olive oil and coriander. Add salt and pepper just before serving. This dish can also be served cold.

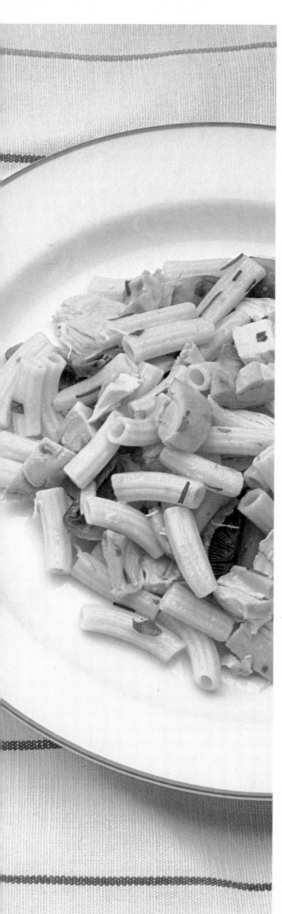

Above: Chicken with peppers
Left: Chicken risotto
Right: Herbed chicken pasta

DEVILLED TURKEY

Preparation time: 10 minutes, plus marinating overnight
Cooking time: 30 minutes
KJ/calorie count: 1045/250

350 g/12 oz cubed turkey meat
2 tablespoons Worcestershire sauce
2 tablespoons lemon juice
1 teaspoon dry mustard
1 teaspoon tabasco
25 g/1 oz butter
1 tablespoon plain flour
300 ml/½ pint skimmed milk
1 red pepper, cored, seeded and cut into strips (optional)
salt
freshly ground black pepper
chopped fresh parsley, to garnish

1. Place the turkey pieces in a shallow dish. Mix together the Worcestershire sauce, lemon juice, mustard and tabasco, add the turkey and leave to marinate overnight.
2. Place the turkey and marinade in a saucepan and simmer for about 25 minutes until tender. (Cooking time depends on the size of the turkey pieces.)
3. Meanwhile, melt the butter in a saucepan and stir in the flour. Cook for 2 minutes, stirring.
4. Remove from the heat and stir in the milk. When blended, return to the heat, bring to the boil and simmer gently for 2 minutes, stirring continuously.
5. Add the turkey pieces, marinade mixture and red pepper, if used. Season and cook for a further 5 minutes, stirring gently.
6. Place in a heated serving dish and sprinkle with parsley.

Top left: Devilled turkey
Top right: Gingered turkey
Bottom left: Curried turkey
Bottom right: Turkey portugaise

CURRIED TURKEY

Preparation time: 10 minutes
Cooking time: about 45 minutes
KJ/calorie count: 880/210, plus 75 g/ 3 oz plain boiled rice: 380/90

100 g/4 oz onions, peeled and sliced
1 tablespoon sunflower oil
1 tablespoon curry powder
350 g/12 oz turkey pieces
1 stock cube, crumbled
450 ml/¾ pint water
1 tablespoon fresh or bottled lime juice
½ tablespoon cornflour (optional)

Curries are always better if left overnight and then reheated.

1. Gently fry the onion in the oil for 5 minutes. Stir in the curry powder and cook for a few minutes.
2. Add the turkey pieces and cook until browned. Stir in the crumbled stock cube, water and lime juice and simmer for about 30 minutes until the turkey is tender. Skim off any fat.
3. If necessary, thicken with the cornflour mixed with a little of the liquid. Serve with plain boiled rice.

TURKEY PORTUGAISE

Preparation time: 10 minutes
Cooking time: 20 minutes
KJ/calorie count: 750/180

4 × 100 g/4 oz turkey fillets
1 garlic clove, peeled and crushed
2 tomatoes, roughly chopped
1 carrot, peeled and very thinly sliced
25 g/1 oz chopped onion
salt
freshly ground black pepper

1. Place each turkey fillet on a piece of foil large enough to cover it. Spread a little crushed garlic on each one.
2. Divide the tomato, carrot and onion between the fillets. Sprinkle over salt and pepper.
3. Wrap the fillets completely in foil and cook in a preheated oven at 220°C, 425°F, Gas Mark 7 for about 20 minutes until tender.
4. Serve in the packages with a tomato or green salad.

GINGERED TURKEY

Preparation time: 10 minutes, plus soaking overnight
Cooking time: 10 minutes
KJ/calorie count: 1045/250

225 g/8 oz dried apricots
1-2 teaspoons ground ginger
4 × 100 g/4 oz turkey fillets

1. Place the apricots in a bowl. Just cover with water and add the ground ginger. Leave to stand overnight.
2. Place the turkey fillets on the grid of a grill pan and spoon over a little of the apricot soaking liquid. Put under a hot grill for about 10 minutes, turning once. If necessary, spoon over more apricot liquid.

3. Meanwhile, simmer the apricots in the rest of the soaking liquid for about 10 minutes.
4. Pour the cooked apricots into a blender and liquidize until smooth.
5. Place the cooked turkey fillets on a heated serving dish and pour the apricot sauce over. Serve with green beans.

TURKEY WITH BROCCOLI

Preparation time: 10 minutes
Cooking time: 25-30 minutes
KJ/calorie count: 1250/300

4 turkey breasts (total weight
   450 g/1 lb)
450 g/1 lb broccoli
salt

SAUCE:
25 g/1 oz butter
1 garlic clove, peeled (optional)
1 dessertspoon cornflour
about 300 ml/½ pint skimmed
   milk
about 300 ml/½ pint chicken stock
1 bay leaf
2 tablespoons sherry (optional)
25 g/1 oz grated Parmesan cheese

1. Place the turkey breasts under a preheated hot grill and cook for about 15 minutes until tender.
2. Meanwhile, cook the broccoli in boiling salted water for about 12 minutes until just tender.
3. Arrange the broccoli on a heated serving dish and place the turkey breasts on top. Keep hot.
4. To make the sauce, melt the butter in a saucepan and add the garlic. Cook gently for a few seconds then stir in the cornflour. Cook for 2 minutes, stirring. Remove the garlic.

5. Add enough skimmed milk and chicken stock to make thin sauce. Add the bay leaf and cook for a few minutes, stirring, until the sauce thickens. Add the sherry if used and remove the bay leaf.
6. Pour over the turkey breasts and broccoli. Sprinkle on the Parmesan cheese and place under a preheated hot grill until lightly browned.

VARIATION:
Use asparagus instead of broccoli.
KJ/calorie count: 1045/250

Top: Turkey with broccoli
Bottom: Turkey mornay

TURKEY MILANESE

Preparation time: 10 minutes
Cooking time: 12 minutes
KJ/calorie count: 1045/250

350 g/12 oz cooked turkey meat
100 g/4 oz pasta
salt
1 × 225 g/8 oz can artichoke hearts,
  drained
2 teaspoons chopped fresh
  oregano or 1 teaspoon dried
  oregano
freshly ground black pepper

1. Cut the turkey into bite-sized pieces.
2. Put the pasta in a saucepan of boiling salted water and cook for about 10 minutes until just cooked but still firm. Drain and return to the saucepan.
3. Add the turkey, drained artichoke hearts and herbs to the pan and place over a gentle heat, stirring, until thoroughly heated through. Taste and adjust the seasoning.
4. Place in a heated serving dish.

TURKEY-STUFFED AUBERGINES

Preparation time: 15 minutes, plus
  draining
Cooking time: 30 minutes
KJ/calorie count: 1045/250

2 large aubergines
lemon juice
salt
100 g/4 oz macaroni, cooked
350 g/12 oz cooked turkey meat,
  cut into chunks, or cooked
  turkey pieces
about 300 ml/½ pint tomato juice
1 teaspoon ground coriander
freshly ground black pepper

Cooked turkey pieces are cut into chunks before packaging and are available from certain delicatessens and food stores.

1. Cut each aubergine in half and sprinkle with lemon juice and salt. Leave to drain for at least 30 minutes.
2. Place each half on a piece of foil large enough to completely enclose it. Wrap the aubergine halves and cook in a preheated oven at 200°C, 400°F, Gas Mark 6 for about 30 minutes.
3. Meanwhile, gently heat the macaroni and turkey meat in the tomato juice, coriander and salt and pepper.
4. When the aubergines are tender, unwrap and carefully scoop out the flesh. Mix with the macaroni and turkey pieces and pile back into the aubergine shells.

TURKEY MORNAY

Preparation time: 10 minutes
Cooking time: 20 minutes
KJ/calorie count: 960/230

225 g/8 oz turkey breasts
lemon juice for basting
25 g/1 oz butter
1 tablespoon plain flour
300 ml/½ pint skimmed milk
50 g/2 oz Cheddar cheese, grated
salt
freshly ground black pepper

1. Place the turkey breasts on the grid of a grill pan and spoon over a little lemon juice. Put under a hot grill for 20 minutes, turning occasionally. If necessary, spoon over more lemon juice.
2. Meanwhile, melt the butter in a saucepan and stir in the flour. Cook for 2 minutes, stirring.
3. Remove from the heat and stir in the milk. When blended, return to the heat, bring to the boil and simmer gently for 2 minutes, stirring continuously.
4. Add the grated cheese and salt and pepper and stir until the cheese has melted.
5. Cut the cooked turkey breasts into small portions and place on a heated serving dish. Pour the sauce over and serve with a salad.

Top: Turkey milanese
Bottom: Turkey-stuffed
aubergines

MEAT

LAMB CHOPS WITH ROSEMARY BUTTER

Preparation time: 10 minutes
Cooking time: about 15 minutes
KJ/calorie count: 1045/250

4 lamb chops
25 g/1 oz butter (see method)
25 ml/1 fl oz water
2 teaspoons chopped fresh
 rosemary or 1 teaspoon dried
 rosemary
salt
freshly ground black pepper

It is best to blend the butter and water together in larger quantities and use as required. The mixture, which has half the calories of butter, keeps in a container in the refrigerator for up to a week.

1. Put the lamb chops under a preheated hot grill and cook for about 15 minutes, turning frequently.
2. Place the butter and water in a blender and liquidize until combined.
3. Put into a small bowl and mix in the rosemary, salt and pepper. Arrange the chops on a heated serving dish and top each with a knob of rosemary-flavoured butter.

LAMB WITH PIQUANT SAUCE

Preparation time: 15 minutes, plus
 marinating
Cooking time: about 10 minutes
KJ/calorie count: 630/150

8 lamb cutlets or 4 lamb chops
2 beef stock cubes
8 tablespoons Worcestershire
 sauce
2 teaspoons chopped fresh
 rosemary or 1 teaspoon dried
 rosemary
1 teaspoon ground coriander
120 ml/4 fl oz water
salt
freshly ground black pepper

1. Put the cutlets or chops in a flameproof dish.
2. Crumble the stock cubes into the Worcestershire sauce and stir in the rosemary and coriander. Pour over the lamb and leave to marinate for at least 3 hours, turning frequently.
3. Remove the lamb from the marinade and cook under a hot grill for 10 minutes or until the lamb is cooked to your taste. Turn the meat frequently spooning over the marinade to prevent burning.
4. Put the rest of the marinade in a saucepan with the water, salt and pepper, and bring to the boil. Arrange the lamb cutlets on a heated serving dish and pour the sauce over.

Top: Lamb chops with rosemary butter
Bottom: Lamb with piquant sauce

SHOULDER OF LAMB STUFFED WITH APRICOTS

Preparation time: 20 minutes, plus soaking
Cooking time: about 1½ hours
KJ/calorie count: 100 g/4 oz meat and 50 g/2 oz stuffing – 1130/270

175 g/6 oz dried apricots
25 g/1 oz chopped onion
2 teaspoons chopped fresh rosemary or 1 teaspoon dried rosemary
75 g/3 oz wholemeal breadcrumbs
1 egg, beaten
salt
freshly ground black pepper
1 × 1.5 kg/3 lb shoulder of lamb, boned

1. Soak the apricots overnight. Drain and reserve the soaking liquid.
2. Roughly chop the apricots, add the onion, rosemary and breadcrumbs.
3. Add the beaten egg to the mixture to bind. Add a little apricot soaking liquid, if necessary, and salt and pepper to taste.

4. Spoon the stuffing into the lamb bone cavity and sew up the edges, using a trussing needle and string, to enclose completely the stuffing.
5. Roast in a preheated oven at 200°C, 400°F, Gas Mark 6 for 1½ hours or until tender.

Top: Eastern lamb
Left: Shoulder of lamb stuffed with apricots
Right: Marrow stuffed with lamb
Right: Lamb kebabs

EASTERN LAMB

Preparation time: 10 minutes
Cooking time: about 1 hour
KJ/calorie count: 1550/370

100 g/4 oz onion, peeled and chopped
1 garlic clove, peeled and crushed
120 ml/4 fl oz tomato juice
750 g/1½ lb lamb fillet pieces (or lamb steak, cut into pieces)
½ teaspoon ground mace
½ teaspoon ground coriander
1 teaspoon chopped fresh rosemary or ½ teaspoon dried rosemary
120 ml/4 fl oz chicken stock
1 tablespoon lemon juice
salt
freshly ground black pepper

1. Put the onion and crushed garlic in a saucepan with the tomato juice. Bring to the boil, then simmer until the onion is softened.
2. Add the lamb pieces and stir in the spices and rosemary. Add the stock, lemon juice, salt and pepper and bring to the boil.
3. Transfer all the ingredients to a casserole dish. Cover and cook in the oven at 160°C, 325°F, Gas Mark 3 for about 30 minutes until tender. (The cooking time depends on the size of the lamb pieces.)
4. Skim off any fat with a spoon or fat whisk, or leave until cold and remove the fat, then reheat.

LAMB KEBABS

Preparation time: 15 minutes, plus marinating
Cooking time: 30 minutes
KJ/calorie count: 1590/380

750 g/1½ lb lamb fillet pieces
1 garlic clove, peeled and crushed
salt
freshly ground black pepper
150 ml/¼ pint plain unsweetened yogurt
8 small onions, peeled
4 small tomatoes
1 large green pepper, cored, seeded and sliced
8 button mushrooms
4 bay leaves
rosemary or parsley sprigs, to garnish

1. Put the lamb pieces in a dish. Stir the garlic, salt and pepper into the yogurt, pour over the lamb and leave to marinate for several hours or overnight.
2. Drain the lamb and thread on to 4 skewers alternating with the onions, tomatoes, pepper, mushrooms and bay leaves.
3. Put the skewers on a wire tray over a roasting tin and cook in a preheated oven at 190°C, 375°F, Gas Mark 5 for about 30 minutes.
4. Garnish with the rosemary or parsley sprigs. If liked, serve with plain boiled rice and the remaining yogurt marinade.

MARROW STUFFED WITH LAMB

Preparation time: 45 minutes, plus marinating
Cooking time: 1-1¼ hours
KJ/calorie count: 175 g/6 oz portion – 1250/300

750 g/1½ lb fillet pieces or lamb steak, finely chopped
120 ml/4 fl oz chicken stock
25 g/1 oz chopped onion
2 teaspoons chopped fresh rosemary or 1 teaspoon dried rosemary
250 ml/8 fl oz tomato juice
salt
freshly ground black pepper
100 g/4 oz long-grain rice
1 medium-sized marrow, skinned, cut lengthways and seeded

1. Put the lamb, stock, chopped onion and rosemary in a saucepan and bring to the boil.
2. Add the tomato juice, salt and pepper and simmer for 15-20 minutes until the mixture thickens.
3. Remove from the heat and leave to marinate overnight. Remove the fat.
4. Put the rice in a saucepan of boiling salted water and cook for about 12 minutes or until just tender.
5. Mix the lamb mixture and rice together and spoon into the marrow halves. Wrap the stuffed marrow in foil and bake in the oven at 200°C, 400°F, Gas Mark 6 for 1-1¼ hours.

STEAK AU POIVRE

Preparation time: 15 minutes
Cooking time: 5-10 minutes
KJ/calorie count: 1045/250

black or green peppercorns, to
    taste
4 × 100 g/4 oz sirloin steaks,
    without fat
SAUCE:
300 ml/½ pint plain unsweetened
    yogurt
2 tablespoons brandy
salt
freshly ground black pepper

1. Beat the peppercorns into the steaks
using a meat mallet or rolling pin – the
number of peppercorns depends on
personal taste.
2. Place the steaks under a preheated hot
grill, turning several times, until cooked
according to taste. Transfer to a heated
serving dish.
3. Put the yogurt into a saucepan and add
the brandy, salt and pepper. Heat gently
until the first bubble appears on the
surface and then pour over the steaks. Do
not heat the sauce any more or it will
curdle.

BEEF STROGANOFF

Preparation time: 10 minutes
Cooking time: 10-15 minutes
KJ/calorie count: 1250/300

150 ml/¼ pint plain unsweetened
    yogurt
1 teaspoon Dijon mustard
salt
freshly ground black pepper
450 g/1 lb beef fillet or sirloin steak
2 large onions, peeled and
    chopped
about 150 ml/¼ pint beef stock
3 dessertspoons dry sherry
100 g/4 oz mushrooms, sliced

1. Mix the yogurt, mustard, salt and
pepper together and set aside.
2. Cut the steak into wafer thin strips.
3. Put the onions in a saucepan with just
enough stock to cover the bottom of the
pan. Add the sherry.
4. Gently cook the onions for about 10
minutes until softened, adding more stock
if necessary. When the onions are
transparent, add the beef and mushrooms
and turn up the heat.
5. Cook for 1 minute, stirring rapidly. (If
the beef is not cut wafer thin, the cooking
time will be longer – about 3-5 minutes.)
6. Remove from the heat and stir in the
yogurt mixture. Serve immediately.

HERB-STUFFED SIRLOIN

Preparation time: 20 minutes
Cooking time: about 1 hour
*KJ/calorie count: 100 g/4 oz portion –
    960/230*

750 g/1½ lb sirloin steak, in one
    piece
2 slices bread
50 g/2 oz grated Parmesan cheese
2 teaspoons chopped fresh mixed
    herbs or 1 teaspoon dried mixed
    herbs
50 g/2 oz finely chopped onion
salt
freshly ground black pepper
1 tablespoon Worcestershire sauce

This dish is good served hot or cold.

1. Beat the steak into a thin strip using a
meat mallet or rolling pin.
2. Dip the bread slices into cold water,
squeeze and break into small pieces. Mix
the bread with the cheese, herbs, onion
and salt and pepper to taste.
3. Sprinkle the steak with Worcestershire
sauce and salt. Spoon the stuffing on to
the steak and spread evenly.
4. Roll up the steak and tie firmly with
string at intervals.
5. Place the beef roll on to a piece of foil
large enough to enclose it and wrap like a
parcel. Cook in a preheated oven at 190°C,
375°F, Gas Mark 5 for about 1 hour.
Remove the string before serving, sliced
crossways.

Herb-stuffed sirloin

STEAK WITH TOMATO & GARLIC SAUCE

Preparation time: 15 minutes
Cooking time: about 10 minutes
KJ/calorie count: 960/230

4 × 100 g/4 oz sirloin or rump
   steaks, trimmed of fat
750 g/1½ lb tomatoes, peeled and
   chopped
3 garlic cloves, peeled and finely
   chopped
1 tablespoon chopped fresh
   oregano or basil or 1 teaspoon
   dried oregano or basil
salt
freshly ground black pepper

1. Beat the steaks with a meat mallet or rolling pin until fairly thin. Place under a preheated hot grill, turning frequently, until cooked according to taste.
2. Meanwhile, put the tomatoes, garlic, herbs, salt and pepper in a saucepan and simmer gently for about 10 minutes, until the tomatoes are just soft.
3. Transfer the steaks to a heated serving dish and pour the sauce over.

Above left: Beef stroganoff
Above right: Steak with tomato and garlic sauce
Top: Steak au poivre

BOEUF EN DAUBE

Preparation time: 10 minutes, plus cooling
Cooking time: about 2¼ hours
KJ/calorie count: 1250/300

4 × 100 g/4 oz rump steaks
2-3 lean bacon rashers, chopped
1 wine glass red wine
1 teaspoon chopped fresh mixed herbs or ½ teaspoon dried mixed herbs
2 carrots, scraped and chopped
2 tomatoes, peeled and chopped
salt
freshly ground black pepper
50 g/2 oz sliced onions
strip of orange peel
300 ml/½ pint beef stock

1. Place the steak under a preheated hot grill and cook for 1 minute on each side. Transfer to a casserole and add all the remaining ingredients.
2. Place in a preheated oven at 240°C, 475°F, Gas Mark 9 for 15 minutes. By this time the casserole should be boiling.
3. Reduce the oven temperature to 160°C, 325°F, Gas Mark 3, cover and cook for 1 hour.
4. Remove from the oven and leave to cool. Remove all the fat from the top of the casserole.
5. Replace in a preheated oven at 180°C, 350°F, Gas Mark 4 for 1 hour, adding more stock if necessary.

CURRIED BEEF CASSEROLE

Preparation time: 10 minutes, plus cooling
Cooking time: 2¼ hours
KJ/calorie count: 1045/250

450 g/1 lb rump beef, cubed
2 onions, peeled and chopped
2 sticks celery, chopped
4 carrots, scraped and chopped
1 teaspoon chopped fresh parsley
600 ml/1 pint water
2 beef stock cubes, crumbled
½ teaspoon mild curry powder
salt
freshly ground black pepper

1. Put all the ingredients in a flameproof casserole and bring to the boil.
2. Cover and simmer gently for 2 hours or until the beef is tender, skimming the fat off when necessary.
3. Leave to cool then remove the fat. Reheat and add salt and pepper to taste.

BEEF & TOMATO CASSEROLE

Preparation time: 10 minutes
Cooking time: 2½ hours
KJ/calorie count: 1250/300

750 g/1½ lb stewing steak, cut into bite-sized pieces
4 sticks celery, chopped
4 carrots, scraped and sliced
4 tomatoes, skinned and chopped
250 ml/8 fl oz tomato juice
1 teaspoon dry mustard
salt
freshly ground black pepper
2 beef stock cubes, crumbled

1. Put the steak in a casserole dish. Add the remaining ingredients and mix well.
2. Cover and cook in a preheated oven at 140°C, 275°F, Gas Mark 1 for about 2½ hours or until the beef is tender.
3. Check occasionally that the casserole is not getting too dry, add a little water if necessary.

CHILLI CON CARNE

Preparation time: 10 minutes
Cooking time: about 1½ hours
KJ/calorie count: 1045/250

450 g/1 lb minced beef
50 g/2 oz sliced onions
1 garlic clove, peeled and crushed
1-3 teaspoons chilli powder
2 tablespoons tomato purée
300 ml/½ pint water
2 × 225 g/8 oz cans red kidney beans, drained
salt
freshly ground black pepper

Chilli powder is very hot and varies in strength according to the manufacturer, so it is best used cautiously.

1. Put the beef, onion, garlic, chilli powder, tomato purée and water in a casserole and bring to the boil.
2. Cover and simmer gently for 1¼ hours, skimming the fat off occasionally.
3. Add the red kidney beans, salt and pepper and simmer for a further 10 minutes. Skim off the fat with a spoon or fat whisk.

BEEF & HORSERADISH

Preparation time: 10 minutes, plus cooling
Cooking time: 1 hour 50 minutes
KJ/calorie count: 1170/280

500 g/1¼ lb minced beef
2 beef stock cubes, crumbled
300 ml/½ pint water
2 tablespoons grated horseradish
salt
freshly ground black pepper

If you have time, it is better to let cooked mince and other fatty meat dishes cool down and then remove all the fat. Skimming off the fat when the mixture is hot does not remove it completely.

1. Put the beef, stock cubes and water in a saucepan and bring to the boil.
2. Cover and simmer gently for 1½ hours. Check occasionally that the beef is not getting too dry, add a little water if necessary.
3. Leave to cool then remove the fat.
4. Stir in the horseradish, bring to the boil and simmer for about 20 minutes. Taste and adjust the seasoning.

Top left: Chilli con carne
Centre: Beef and tomato casserole
Top right: Beef and horseradish
Below left: Curried beef casserole
Below right: Boeuf en daube

PORK & PRUNE CASSEROLE

*Preparation time: 10 minutes, plus
soaking*
Cooking time: 1¼ hours
KJ/calorie count: 1500/360

20 stoned prunes, soaked
    overnight
4 × 175 g/6 oz pork chops,
    trimmed of all fat
1 chicken stock cube, crumbled
salt
freshly ground black pepper
1 teaspoon dry mustard
1 tablespoon wine vinegar

1. Put a layer of prunes on the bottom of a
casserole dish.
2. Arrange the pork chops on top. Add
the remaining ingredients and enough of
the prunes soaking liquid to cover.
3. Place in a preheated oven at 220°C,
425°F, Gas Mark 7 for 15 minutes.
4. Lower the temperature to 160°C, 325°F,
Gas Mark 3 for about 1 hour until the
chops are tender.

GAMMON & BROAD BEANS

Preparation time: 10 minutes
Cooking time: about 40 minutes
KJ/calorie count: 1045/250

225 g/8 oz shelled broad beans
salt
25 g/1 oz butter
25 g/1 oz plain flour
350 g/12 oz cooked gammon, cut
　into bite-sized pieces
freshly ground black pepper
½ teaspoon grated nutmeg

1. Cook the beans in boiling salted water for about 15 minutes. Drain and reserve the cooking liquid.
2. Melt the butter in a saucepan and add the flour. Cook gently for 2 minutes.
3. Stir in about 300 ml/½ pint of the beans cooking liquid and cook for a few minutes until thickened.
4. Add the gammon and heat gently until warmed through, stirring frequently.
5. Add more of the beans cooking liquid if the mixture is too thick. Taste and adjust the seasoning.
6. Add the beans and transfer to a heated serving dish. Sprinkle with the nutmeg.

PORK NORMANDY

Preparation time: 10 minutes
Cooking time: 1¼ hours
KJ/calorie count: 1250/300

1 large cooking apple, cored and
　cut into chunks
4 × 175 g/6 oz pork chops,
　trimmed of all fat
100 g/4 oz onions, peeled and
　sliced
1 tablespoon chopped fresh sage
　or 1 teaspoon dried sage
salt
freshly ground black pepper
250 ml/8 fl oz unsweetened apple
　juice

1. Put the apple pieces on the bottom of a casserole dish.
2. Arrange the pork chops on top and sprinkle over the sliced onion, sage and salt and pepper. Pour over the apple juice.
3. Cook in a preheated oven at 220°C, 425°F, Gas Mark 7 for 15 minutes.
4. Lower the temperature to 160°C, 325°F, Gas Mark 3 for about 1 hour or until the chops are tender.

PORK WITH ORANGE & JUNIPER

Preparation time: 10 minutes, plus
*　marinating*
Cooking time: 10-15 minutes
KJ/calorie count: 920/220

4 × 100 g/4 oz pork fillets, trimmed
　of fat
300 ml/½ pint unsweetened
　orange juice
12-20 juniper berries
salt
freshly ground black pepper

1. Place the fillets in a dish and pour the orange juice over.
2. Crush the juniper berries with the back of a spoon and add to the orange juice with the salt and pepper. Cover and leave to marinate for at least 5 hours.
3. Remove the fillets and place under a preheated hot grill. Cook for 10-15 minutes, turning frequently and spooning over some of the orange marinade to prevent burning.
4. Strain the remaining orange marinade and pour into a saucepan. Bring to the boil and boil briskly to reduce slightly.
5. Arrange the pork on a heated serving dish and pour the orange sauce over.

Back left: Pork and prune casserole
Back right: Gammon and broad beans
Front left: Pork Normandy
Front right: Pork with orange and juniper

VEAL PAPRIKA

Preparation time: 10 minutes
Cooking time: about 10 minutes
KJ/calorie count: 920/220

---

4 × 175 g/6 oz pieces fillet of veal
1 tablespoon lemon juice
4 tablespoons tomato purée
3 teaspoons paprika
300 ml/½ pint plain unsweetened
    yogurt
salt
freshly ground black pepper

1. Put the veal fillets on the rack of a grill pan. Cook under a fairly hot grill for about 5 minutes on each side (depending on the thickness of the fillets), spooning over lemon juice to prevent burning.
2. Mix together the tomato purée, paprika and remaining lemon juice and heat gently.
3. Remove from the heat and stir in the yogurt and salt and pepper to taste.
4. Put the fillets of veal on to a heated serving plate and pour the sauce over.

VARIATION:
This sauce is rather sharp. If you prefer a slightly sweeter sauce, add 3-6 crushed artificial sweetener tablets, depending on taste, just before serving.

ITALIAN VEAL

Preparation time: 20 minutes
Cooking time: about 20 minutes
KJ/calorie count: 920/220

---

10 anchovy fillets
12 capers
salt
freshly ground black pepper
8 thin slices fillet of veal

1. Pound the anchovies and capers together with salt and pepper, using a pestle and mortar or the back of a wooden spoon.
2. Put 4 veal fillets on pieces of foil large enough to enclose them. Spread with the anchovy and caper mixture. Lay a second veal fillet on top.

3. Wrap the fillets in the foil. Cook in a preheated oven at 220°C, 425°F, Gas Mark 7 for 20 minutes or until the veal is tender. Serve with a tomato and onion salad.

Right: Veal with garlic
and tomatoes
Far right: Veal and
courgette casserole

VEAL WITH GARLIC & TOMATOES

Preparation time: 15 minutes
Cooking time: about 20 minutes
KJ/calorie count: 840/200

4 × 175 g/6 oz pieces fillet of veal
2 tomatoes, skinned and chopped
2 garlic cloves, peeled and crushed
1 stick celery, finely chopped
salt
freshly ground black pepper

1. Put the veal fillets on pieces of foil large enough to enclose them.
2. Mix together the tomatoes, garlic and celery, and spoon over the veal.
3. Season with salt and pepper and then wrap the fillets in the foil.
4. Cook in a preheated oven at 220°C, 425°F, Gas Mark 7 for about 20 minutes or until the veal is tender.

VEAL & COURGETTE CASSEROLE

Preparation time: 10 minutes, plus
*   draining*
Cooking time: about 40 minutes
KJ/calorie count: 840/200

450 g/1 lb courgettes, thinly sliced
salt
450 g/1 lb lean veal, sliced or cubed
freshly ground black pepper
pinch of ground nutmeg
2 tablespoons stock
50 g/2 oz Parmesan cheese, grated

Use any lean cut of veal, such as pie veal, for this recipe.

1. Sprinkle the courgette slices with salt and leave to drain for 1-2 hours.
2. Place a layer of courgettes in a casserole dish, cover with a layer of veal. Repeat the layers until all the veal and courgettes have been used, ending with courgettes.
3. Add salt, pepper, nutmeg and stock. Sprinkle with the Parmesan cheese.
4. Cook in a preheated oven at 200°C, 400°F, Gas Mark 6 for about 40 minutes or until the veal is tender.

Far left: Veal paprika
Left: Italian veal

VITELLO TONNATO

Preparation time: 15 minutes, plus chilling
KJ/calorie count: 1250/300

350 g/12 oz lean roast veal
1 × 200 g/7 oz can tuna fish, drained
2-3 anchovy fillets, drained
1 tablespoon sherry
1 tablespoon low-calorie mayonnaise
salt
freshly ground black pepper
1 tablespoon chopped capers, to garnish (optional)

The best way to roast veal for this dish is to place the meat on a rack over a roasting dish half-filled with water. Roast in a preheated oven at 200°C, 400°F, Gas Mark 6 for 20 minutes per 450 g/1 lb, plus 20 minutes. Baste with water frequently.

1. Slice the roast veal thinly and trim off any fat.
2. Place the tuna fish, anchovies, sherry, mayonnaise, salt and pepper in a blender and liquidize until smooth.
3. Pour over the veal and chill slightly.
4. Alternatively, liquidize the ingredients until they are combined but still a thick consistency. Place a spoonful in the centre of each veal slice and roll up. Chill slightly.
5. Scatter over chopped capers, if using, before serving.

STUFFED BREAST OF VEAL

Preparation time: 15 minutes
Cooking time: about 1½ hours
*KJ/calorie count: 1090/260 per 100 g/
    4 oz serving*

1 kg/2 lb breast of veal, boned
4 eggs, beaten
salt
freshly ground black pepper
4 slices lean ham
1-2 teaspoons chopped fresh
    tarragon or ½-1 teaspoon dried
    tarragon

This dish looks pretty carved and included in a buffet spread.

1. Unroll the veal and flatten out if necessary. Remove as much fat as possible.
2. Season the eggs with salt and pepper. Pour into a non-stick omelette or small frying pan, or ordinary pan using a little low-calorie oil spray, and make an omelette (see page 37).
3. Place the open omelette on the veal. It will be necessary to trim the omelette and put the side pieces on top.
4. Lay the slices of ham over the omelette, again trimming to fit the veal. Sprinkle with the tarragon.
5. Roll up the veal and tie at intervals with string. Place in a roasting tin and roast in a preheated oven at 200°C, 400°F, Gas Mark 6 for about 1½ hours, basting and turning frequently. Serve hot or cold.

LEMON & TARRAGON VEAL

Preparation time: 10 minutes
Cooking time: 2 hours
KJ/calorie count: 1250/300

1 kg/2 lb pie veal, cut into bite-
    sized pieces
1 wineglass white wine
1 wineglass lemon juice
2 teaspoons chopped fresh
    tarragon or 1 teaspoon dried
salt
freshly ground black pepper
about 150 ml/¼ pint chicken stock

1. Put the veal in a casserole dish with the remaining ingredients except the stock.
2. Pour in just enough stock to cover the veal.
3. Cover and cook in a preheated oven at 150°C, 300°F, Gas Mark 2 for about 2 hours or until the veal is tender. Serve with mange-tout peas.

VEAL WITH PINEAPPLE

*Preparation time: 10 minutes, plus
    cooling*
Cooking time: 1½ hours
KJ/calorie count: 1130/270

750 g/1½ lb lean pie veal, cubed
300 ml/½ pint chicken stock
salt
freshly ground black pepper
175 ml/6 fl oz orange juice
½ medium pineapple, peeled and
    cut into chunks

1. Place the veal in a saucepan with the stock and bring to the boil. Add salt and pepper, cover and simmer for about 30 minutes.
2. Leave to cool, then skim off all the fat.
3. Transfer to a casserole dish and add the orange juice and pineapple. Cover and cook in a preheated oven at 200°C, 400°F, Gas Mark 6 for 1 hour or until tender.

Top back: Stuffed breast of veal
**Top left: Lemon and
tarragon veal**
Top right: Veal with pineapple
Left: Vitello tonnato

SWEETBREADS IN LEMON SAUCE

*Preparation time: about 30 minutes,
    plus soaking*
Cooking time: 45 minutes
KJ/calorie count: 940/225

500 g/1¼ lb lamb's sweetbreads
1 tablespoon lemon juice
salt
freshly ground black pepper
1 large red pepper, cored, seeded
    and thinly sliced
25 g/1 oz butter
15 g/½ oz plain flour
1 tablespoon dried skimmed milk
    powder

1. Soak the sweetbreads in cold water for 1 hour.
2. Discard the water. Put the sweetbreads in a saucepan and add water to cover. Bring to the boil, then drain. Put the sweetbreads back in the pan, add fresh water and poach gently for about 10 minutes, skimming as necessary.
3. Add the lemon juice and salt and pepper. Cover the saucepan tightly and simmer for 30 minutes or until the sweetbreads are tender.
4. Blanch the red pepper strips in boiling water for 1 minute.
5. Drain the sweetbreads, reserving the cooking liquid. Allow them to cool slightly then remove the skins. Keep warm in a heated serving dish.
6. Melt the butter in a saucepan and stir in the flour. Cook for 2 minutes.
7. Stir in the sweetbreads cooking liquid, red pepper and skimmed milk powder. Add salt and pepper to taste and cook for a few minutes.
8. Pour the sauce over the sweetbreads and serve.

KIDNEY & MUSHROOM CASSEROLE

Preparation time: 15 minutes
Cooking time: about 40 minutes
KJ/calorie count: 710/170

450 g/1 lb lamb's kidneys, skinned
    and cored
100 g/4 oz onions, peeled and
    sliced
300 ml/½ pint beef stock
120 ml/4 fl oz sherry
salt
freshly ground black pepper
225 g/8 oz mushrooms, stalks
    removed, sliced if large

1. Slice or halve the kidneys. Place under a preheated hot grill and cook for 1 minute on each side.
2. Transfer to a casserole dish and add the onions, stock, sherry, salt and pepper. Stir in the mushrooms.
3. Cover and cook in a preheated oven at 200°C, 400°F, Gas Mark 6 for about 40 minutes or until the kidneys are tender. Serve with plain boiled rice.

LIVER KEBABS

Preparation time: 15 minutes
Cooking time: 20 minutes
KJ/calorie count: 1045/250

450 g/1 lb lamb's liver, cut into
    bite-sized pieces
4 onions, peeled and quartered
4 tomatoes, quartered
100 g/4 oz mushrooms
8 bay leaves
salt
freshly ground black pepper
lemon juice

1. Thread the liver pieces, onion, tomato, mushrooms and bay leaves alternately on to 4 skewers.
2. Sprinkle with salt and pepper.
3. Cook under a preheated hot grill for about 20 minutes turning occasionally and spooning over the lemon juice to prevent burning.

**Top left: Sweetbreads in
lemon sauce
Centre: Curried kidneys
Top right: Kidney and
mushroom casserole
Right: Liver kebabs
Far right: Braised liver**

CURRIED KIDNEYS

Preparation time: 10 minutes
Cooking time: about 30 minutes
KJ/calorie count: 670/160

450 g/1 lb lamb's kidneys, cored and diced
100 g/4 oz onions, peeled and chopped
2 garlic cloves, peeled and crushed
250 ml/8 fl oz tomato juice
1 tablespoon curry powder
1 tablespoon lime or lemon juice
salt
freshly ground black pepper
beef stock (if necessary)

1. Put all the ingredients except the beef stock in a non-stick saucepan.
2. Bring to the boil, cover and simmer for about 30 minutes.
3. Check occasionally that the kidney mixture is not getting too dry, add a little beef stock if necessary.

BRAISED LIVER

Preparation time: 10 minutes
Cooking time: 30 minutes
KJ/calorie count: 840/200 for chicken livers; 1090/260 for lamb's liver

450 g/1 lb chicken livers or lamb's liver, cut into pieces
1 large cooking apple, cored and cut into chunks
50 g/2 oz sliced onion
350 ml/12 fl oz tomato juice
2 teaspoons Worcestershire sauce
salt
freshly ground black pepper

1. Put the liver in a casserole dish. Add the apple and sliced onion.
2. Pour in the tomato juice, Worcestershire sauce and add salt and pepper.
3. Cover and cook in a preheated oven at 180°C, 350°F, Gas Mark 4 for about 30 minutes.

VEGETABLES

BEETROOT SOUFFLÉ

Preparation time: 15 minutes
Cooking time: about 25 minutes
KJ/calorie count: 920/220

450 g/1 lb cooked beetroots, skinned and diced
1 teaspoon dry mustard
175 ml/6 fl oz orange juice
3 tablespoons cornflour
4 eggs, separated

1. Place the beetroot in a blender with the mustard and half the orange juice and liquidize to a purée.
2. Mix the remaining orange juice with the cornflour and heat gently until the mixture thickens. Add to the blender and liquidize until smooth.
3. Beat the egg yolks, one by one, into the mixture. Whisk the egg whites until very stiff and fold into the mixture.
4. Put into a soufflé dish and bake in a preheated oven at 220°C, 425°F, Gas Mark 7 for 20-25 minutes until risen. Serve immediately.

VARIATION:
Substitute 225 g/8 oz cooked carrots for the beetroot. Increase the orange juice to 250 ml/8 fl oz and make in the same way, flavouring with mace instead of mustard.

VEGETABLE KEBABS

Preparation time: 15 minutes
Cooking time: about 20 minutes
KJ/calorie count: 400/95, plus rice

1 medium onion, peeled and quartered
4 courgettes, thickly sliced
4 tomatoes, skinned and quartered
8 button mushrooms, thickly sliced
1 medium eating apple, cored and cut into eighths
8 bay leaves
unsweetened apple juice, to baste
salt
freshly ground black pepper

1. Boil the onion quarters for about 5 minutes until tender but still firm.
2. Boil the courgette slices for 1-2 minutes to soften.
3. Thread the onion, tomatoes, mushrooms, courgettes, apple and bay leaves on to 4 skewers and place under a preheated hot grill. Turn frequently, basting with seasoned apple juice, for 10-15 minutes until cooked.
4. Serve on a bed of rice.

Top left: Beetroot soufflé
Top right: Vegetable kebabs
Bottom: Baked onion

BAKED ONIONS

Preparation time: 10 minutes
Cooking time: 1 hour
KJ/calorie count: 840/200, plus rice

4 large onions, peeled and halved
75 g/3 oz wholemeal breadcrumbs
4 dessertspoons crunchy peanut butter

1. Scoop out the centres of the onions and chop finely. Mix with the breadcrumbs and then combine with the peanut butter.
2. Spoon the mixture into the onion cavities. Reform the onions and wrap in foil.
3. Cook in a preheated oven at 200°C, 400°F, Gas Mark 6 for about 1 hour until tender.
4. Serve with plain boiled rice.

SPINACH & CHEESE QUICHE

Preparation time: 15 minutes
Cooking time: 20-25 minutes
KJ/calorie count: 960/230

450 g/1 lb spinach, washed and trimmed
3 eggs, beaten
600 ml/1 pint skimmed milk
salt
freshly ground black pepper
pinch of grated nutmeg (optional)
100 g/4 oz Cheddar or Gruyère cheese, grated

1. Pick over and reserve about 16 of the best spinach leaves.
2. Cook the rest of the spinach for about 5 minutes, using only the water remaining on the leaves. If very young, it is not necessary to cook the spinach.
3. Arrange 8 of the reserved leaves on the base of a flan dish. Arrange the remaining reserved leaves overlapping the sides of the dish.
4. Beat the eggs with the skimmed milk, adding salt, pepper, nutmeg, if used, and grated cheese.
5. Put the partly cooked spinach into the flan case and pour over the egg mixture. Fold the spinach leaves over the top to cover completely the filling.
6. Bake in a preheated oven at 200°C, 400°F, Gas Mark 6 for about 20 minutes or until the quiche is set. It may be necessary to cover the spinach leaves with foil towards the end of cooking to prevent burning.

VEGETABLE MORNAY

Preparation time: 10 minutes
Cooking time: 15 minutes
KJ/calorie count: 1045/250

15 g/½ oz butter
15 g/½ oz plain flour
300 ml/½ pint skimmed milk
100 g/4 oz cheese, grated
salt
freshly ground black pepper
450 g/1 lb mixed cooked vegetables, e.g. carrots, peas, parsnips, cauliflower, celery, diced

1. Melt the butter in a saucepan and add the flour. Cook for 2 minutes, stirring.
2. Gradually add enough milk to make a fairly thick sauce.
3. Stir in the cheese, and salt and pepper to taste. When the cheese begins to melt, add the cooked vegetables and cook, stirring, for 5 minutes.
4. Alternatively, sprinkle with 50 g/2 oz of the cheese and place under a preheated hot grill until lightly browned.

GINGERED CARROTS

Preparation time: 10 minutes
Cooking time: 20 minutes
KJ/calorie count: 125/30

450 g/1 lb carrots, peeled and thinly sliced
about 300 ml/½ pint unsweetened orange juice
about 300 ml/½ pint chicken stock
1 teaspoon ground ginger
½ teaspoon ground mace
salt
freshly ground black pepper

1. Place the carrots in a saucepan and cover with the orange juice and stock.
2. Add the spices and salt and pepper, bring to the boil and simmer gently for about 20 minutes until tender.
3. Drain off any excess liquid, then turn into a heated serving dish.

Top: Spinach and cheese quiche
Centre: Vegetable mornay
Bottom: Gingered carrots

BAKED POTATO AND ONION LAYER

Preparation time: 15 minutes
Cooking time: about 1 hour
KJ/calorie count: 630/150 per 225 g/
* 8 oz serving*

4 medium potatoes, peeled and
  finely sliced
4 medium onions, peeled and
  finely sliced
salt
freshly ground black pepper
1 garlic clove, peeled and crushed
1-2 teaspoons chopped fresh sage
  or ½-1 teaspoon dried sage
about 175 ml/6 fl oz skimmed milk

1. Arrange the potato and onion slices in alternate layers in a shallow ovenproof dish, sprinkling salt, pepper, garlic and sage between each layer.
2. Pour over the skimmed milk – it should come about two-thirds of the way up the sides. Cover and bake in a preheated oven at 200°C, 400°F, Gas Mark 6 for about 50 minutes.
3. Uncover to allow the top to brown, then cook for a further 10 minutes. If the dish becomes too dry during cooking add a little more milk, but the finished dish should have absorbed all the milk.

POTATO CAKES

Preparation time: 15 minutes
Cooking time: about 5 minutes
KJ/calorie count: fried – 890/220,
* grilled – 840/200*

450 g/1 lb cooked potato, mashed
100 g/4 oz cheese, grated
1 egg, beaten
1 tablespoon skimmed milk
25 g/1 oz finely chopped onion
salt
freshly ground black pepper
low-calorie oil for frying (see
  method)

1. Mix the mashed potato and grated cheese together.
2. Beat the egg with the skimmed milk and slowly add to the potato mixture, making sure it does not become too moist. Add the chopped onion and salt and pepper to taste.
3. Shape into eight little cakes.
4. Spray a frying pan with low-calorie oil and fry the cakes on both sides until brown. Alternatively, place under a preheated hot grill until browned on both sides, spraying with a little oil if necessary.

VEGETABLE-STUFFED MARROW

Preparation time: 10 minutes, plus
* parsnip purée*
Cooking time: 25-30 minutes
KJ/calorie count: 460/110 per 225 g/
* 8 oz serving*

1 medium marrow, peeled
salt
freshly ground black pepper or
  pinch of curry powder
Parsnip Purée (page 113)

1. Cut the marrow in half lengthways and scoop out the seeds.
2. Add salt and pepper or curry powder to the parsnip purée and spoon into the marrow cavities.
3. Reform the marrow and wrap in foil.
4. Cook in a preheated oven at 200°C, 400°F, Gas Mark 6 for 30-45 minutes until tender. Unwrap and cut into slices for serving.

VARIATION:
Substitute Ratatouille (page 109), well drained, for the Parsnip Purée and omit the curry powder.
KJ/calorie count: 380/90

Top: Baked potato and
onion layer
Centre: Potato cakes
Bottom: Vegetable-stuffed
marrow

JELLIED TOMATO RING

Preparation time: 10 minutes, plus setting
Cooking time: 5 minutes
KJ/calorie count: 190/45

4 tomatoes, skinned and sliced
600 ml/1 pint tomato juice
1 teaspoon Worcestershire sauce
salt
freshly ground black pepper
15 g/½ oz powdered gelatine
1 bunch watercress

1. Arrange the tomato slices in the base of a 19 cm/7½ inch ring mould.
2. Heat the tomato juice and stir in the Worcestershire sauce, salt and pepper. Sprinkle in the gelatine and heat gently, stirring until the gelatine has dissolved.
3. Pour into the ring and place in the refrigerator or a cool place and leave to set for about 3 hours. Turn out carefully and fill the centre with watercress.

ORIENTAL VEGETABLES

Preparation time: 10 minutes
Cooking time: 15-20 minutes
KJ/calorie count: 145/35

450 g/1 lb mixed vegetables, e.g.
    cauliflower, onions,
    mushrooms, leeks, fennel
1 wine glass white wine
1 wine glass wine vinegar
1 teaspoon ground coriander
1 teaspoon ground mace
1 teaspoon dried rosemary
salt
artificial liquid sweetener, to taste
    (optional)

1. Cut the cauliflower into florets, the peeled onions into quarters or eighths depending on size, the leeks and fennel into slices.
2. Place all the vegetables in a saucepan with the white wine, vinegar, spices, rosemary and salt. Add enough water to cover, bring to the boil and simmer gently for 15-20 minutes. The vegetables should be slightly crisp.
3. When cooked, taste, and if very sharp add artificial sweetener to taste. Serve hot or cold.

CUCUMBER MOULD

Preparation time: 20 minutes, plus setting
KJ/calorie count: 250/60

15 g/½ oz powdered gelatine
250 ml/8 fl oz lemon juice
250 ml/8 fl oz hot water
artificial liquid sweetener, to taste
    (optional)
1 cucumber, peeled and sliced
225 g/8 oz grapes, seeded

1. Sprinkle the gelatine on to the lemon juice and allow to soften. Add to the hot water and stir until the gelatine has dissolved. Add artificial sweetener to taste, if used.
2. Place about half the cucumber slices in a 19 cm/7½ inch mould with the grapes. Pour over the lemon jelly mixture.
3. Arrange the remaining cucumber slices on top of the mould in a pattern. Place in the refrigerator or a cool place and leave to set for about 3 hours. Turn out and serve.

CHICORY & CUCUMBER MOULD.

Preparation time: 20 minutes, plus setting
KJ/calorie count: 440/105

1 or 2 heads chicory
225 g/8 oz curd cheese
1 cucumber, peeled and sliced
1 bunch spring onions, trimmed
    and finely chopped
15 g/½ oz powdered gelatine
75 ml/3 fl oz water

1. Separate the chicory leaves.
2. Put the curd cheese, cucumber and onions in a blender.
3. Sprinkle the gelatine over the water in a teacup, stand the cup in a bowl of hot water and stir until dissolved. Add the dissolved gelatine to the mixture in the blender and liquidize until smooth.
4. Pour into a deep 18 cm/7 inch cake tin with a spring clip.
5. Put the chicory leaves round the inside edge of the tin in an upright position so that they form a circle enclosing the curd cheese mixture.
6. Place in the refrigerator or a cool place and leave to set for about 3 hours. Carefully release the spring clip and lift off the tin.

CARROT & ASPARAGUS MOULD

Preparation time: 15 minutes, plus setting
KJ/calorie count: 145/35

225 g/8 oz cooked sliced carrots
600 ml/1 pint jellied chicken stock or 600 ml/1 pint hot water with 15 g/½ oz powdered gelatine and 1 chicken stock cube
1 × 275 g/10 oz can asparagus, drained

1. Arrange some of the carrots in the base and around the sides of a straight sided 600 ml/1 pint dish.
2. Pour over the jellied stock. To make jellied stock, sprinkle the powdered gelatine and crumbled stock cube into the hot water and stir until the gelatine has dissolved.
3. Cut up the asparagus and arrange in the centre. Place a pattern of carrot slices on top of the jellied stock.

4. Place in the refrigerator or a cool place and leave to set for about 3 hours. Turn out and serve.

Top left: Jellied tomato ring
Top right: Carrot and asparagus mould
Centre: Oriental vegetables
Bottom left: Cucumber mould
Bottom right: Chicory and cucumber mould

KIDNEY BEAN CASSEROLE

Preparation time: 10 minutes
Cooking time: about 10 minutes
KJ/calorie count: 710/170 per 100 g/
*   4 oz serving*

---

2 × 275 g/10 oz cans red kidney
    beans, drained and rinsed
2 medium onions, peeled and
    sliced
2 rashers bacon, fat removed,
    chopped
about 300 ml/½ pint chicken stock
salt
freshly ground black pepper

1. Place the kidney beans, onions and
bacon in a saucepan.
2. Pour over just enough stock to cover
and add salt and pepper. Simmer gently
for about 10 minutes or until the onions
are tender. Turn into a heated serving
dish.

VARIATION:
Use 450 g/1 lb dried kidney beans instead
of canned. Soak overnight. Drain the
beans, cover with water, bring to the boil,
then boil rapidly for at least 10 minutes.
Cover and simmer for about 3 hours until
soft.

VEGETABLE HOT POT

Preparation time: 20 minutes
Cooking time: 25 minutes
KJ/calorie count: 420/100

---

4 medium carrots, scraped and
    sliced
4 medium parsnips, peeled and
    sliced
2 medium turnips, peeled and
    sliced
2 medium onions, peeled and
    sliced
600 ml/1 pint chicken stock or
    water with 2 chicken stock
    cubes
salt
freshly ground black pepper
1 bay leaf
1 tablespoon chopped fresh
    parsley

1. Place the vegetables in a flameproof
casserole with the stock, salt, pepper, bay
leaf and parsley.
2. Bring to the boil, skim, then cover and
simmer for about 25 minutes or until all
the vegetables are tender.
3. Serve straight from the casserole.

Top: Vegetable hotpot
Bottom: Broccoli au gratin

Left: Kidney bean casserole
Centre: Corn and butter bean
casserole
Right: Broad bean and green
pea casserole

CORN & BUTTER BEAN CASSEROLE

Preparation time: 10 minutes
Cooking time: 20 minutes
KJ/calorie count: 840/200

1 × 300 g/11 oz can sweetcorn
  kernels
1 × 425 g/15 oz can butter beans,
  drained
1 tablespoon cornflour
scant 600 ml/1 pint skimmed milk
½ teaspoon caraway seeds
salt
freshly ground black pepper

1. Drain the sweetcorn, reserving the liquid. Place the sweetcorn and butter beans in a saucepan.
2. Mix the cornflour and skimmed milk together and heat gently. Add the liquid from the can of sweetcorn and stir until the mixture thickens. Add the caraway seeds and salt and pepper to taste.
3. Pour the sauce over the vegetables, cover and cook for about 15 minutes, then turn into a heated serving dish.

BROAD BEAN & GREEN PEA CASSEROLE

Preparation time: 15 minutes
Cooking time: about 25 minutes
KJ/calorie count: 790/190

450 g/1 lb green peas, shelled
  weight
450 g/1 lb broad beans, shelled
  weight
salt
1 tablespoon cornflour
300 ml/½ pint skimmed milk
300 ml/½ pint stock or vegetable
  cooking liquid (see method)
pinch of dried rosemary
freshly ground black pepper

1. Place the peas and beans together in a saucepan of boiling salted water and cook for about 15 minutes until tender. Drain, reserving the cooking liquid.
2. Mix the cornflour and skimmed milk together and heat gently, stirring, adding 300 ml/½ pint vegetable cooking liquid or stock, rosemary and salt and pepper to taste. Add the peas and beans and heat together for about 2 minutes, then turn into a heated serving dish.

BROCCOLI AU GRATIN

Preparation time: 10 minutes
Cooking time: 25-30 minutes
KJ/calorie count: 1170/280

1 medium onion, peeled and
  sliced
1 green pepper, cored, seeded and
  sliced
1 kg/2 lb broccoli
2 tablespoons cornflour
600 ml/1 pint skimmed milk
100 g/4 oz Cheddar cheese, grated
pinch of grated nutmeg (optional)
salt
freshly ground black pepper

1. Place the onion, pepper and broccoli in a saucepan of boiling water. Cover and cook for about 15 minutes until tender.
2. Mix the cornflour with the skimmed milk. Pour into a saucepan and heat gently, stirring. Add 50 g/2 oz of the cheese and when thickened, add the nutmeg, if using, and salt and pepper to taste.
3. Transfer the drained broccoli and pepper mixture to a heated gratin dish and pour over the sauce.
4. Sprinkle with the remaining cheese and place under a preheated hot grill until the cheese melts.

GLOBE ARTICHOKES

KJ/calorie count: 100/25 per average artichoke

Globe artichokes are excellent served simply with a vinaigrette dressing but are also delicious stuffed.

To prepare globe artichokes for cooking, remove the tough outer leaves and cut away the stalk. Wash well under running water. Place the artichoke heads in a large saucepan of boiling salted water and simmer for 25-40 minutes, depending on size. When tender, a leaf will pull out easily. Turn the artichokes upside down in a colander to drain. Leave to cool. Remove the hairy 'choke' from the centre of each artichoke with your fingers, a spoon or knife.

GLOBE ARTICHOKES WITH RUSSIAN SALAD

Preparation time: 20 minutes
KJ/calorie count: 500/120

100 g/4 oz ham, diced
100 g/4 oz cooked peas
100 g/4 oz cooked carrots, diced
100 g/4 oz cooked green beans, diced
100 g/4 oz cooked beetroot, diced
100 g/4 oz cooked potatoes, diced
50 g/2 oz low-calorie mayonnaise
salt
freshly ground black pepper
4 globe artichokes, cooked

1. Stir the ham and vegetables into the mayonnaise and mix well. Add salt and pepper to taste and mix again.
2. Remove the chokes from the artichokes and push back the leaves to make room for the stuffing. If necessary, remove a few of the inner leaves.
3. Spoon the Russian salad into the centre of the artichokes.

GLOBE ARTICHOKES WITH MUSHROOM & TOMATO STUFFING

Preparation time: 10 minutes
Cooking time: about 20 minutes
KJ/calorie count: 670/160

100 g/4 oz long-grain rice
100 g/4 oz onions, peeled and sliced
1 stock cube, crumbled
225 g/8 oz tomatoes, skinned and quartered
100 g/4 oz mushrooms
100 g/4 oz ham, chopped
1 teaspoon chopped fresh parsley
1 teaspoon chopped fresh thyme
salt
freshly ground black pepper
4 globe artichokes, cooked

1. Place the rice in a saucepan of boiling water with the sliced onion and stock cube added. Cook for about 12 minutes until just tender.
2. Add the tomatoes and mushrooms and cook for a further 5 minutes. Drain. Stir in the ham, herbs and salt and pepper to taste.
3. Remove the chokes from the artichokes and push back the leaves to make room for the stuffing. If necessary, remove a few of the inner leaves.
4. Spoon the mushroom and tomato mixture into the centre of the artichokes.

Top: Globe artichoke with Russian salad
Bottom: Globe artichoke with mushroom and tomato stuffing

MUSHROOMS A LA GRECQUE

Preparation time: 5 minutes, plus cooling
Cooking time: 15 minutes
KJ/calorie count: 80/20

450 g/1 lb button mushrooms
25 g/1 oz chopped onion
150 ml/¼ pint tomato juice
50 ml/2 fl oz lemon juice
½ teaspoon dried basil
1 garlic clove, peeled and crushed
½ teaspoon ground coriander
salt
freshly ground black pepper
1 tablespoon chopped fresh parsley, to garnish

1. Place all the ingredients together in a saucepan.
2. Bring to the boil and simmer for about 15 minutes until the mushrooms have absorbed all the liquid.
3. Transfer to a serving dish and leave to cool. Sprinkle with chopped parsley just before serving.

COURGETTES LYONNAISE

Preparation time: 10 minutes
Cooking time: about 15 minutes
KJ/calorie count: 80/20

1 garlic clove, peeled and crushed
100 g/4 oz onion, peeled and chopped
150 ml/¼ pint chicken or vegetable stock
salt
450 g/1 lb courgettes, sliced
freshly ground black pepper

1. Stir the garlic and onion into the stock. Add salt and bring to the boil.
2. Add the courgettes, cover and simmer for 10-15 minutes until tender. Taste and adjust the seasoning. Serve hot or cold.

VARIATION:
Use sliced leeks instead of courgettes.
KJ/calorie count: 110/26

RATATOUILLE

Preparation time: 15 minutes
Cooking time: 20 minutes
KJ/calorie count: 500/120

4 courgettes, sliced
4 tomatoes, skinned and quartered
2 medium aubergines, sliced
2 onions, peeled and sliced
2 large red peppers, cored, seeded and sliced
2 bay leaves
300 ml/½ pint tomato juice
salt
freshly ground black pepper

1. Place all the vegetables in a saucepan with the bay leaves, tomato juice, salt and pepper.
2. Bring to the boil and skim. Cover and simmer for about 20 minutes or until all the vegetables are tender.
3. If there is still too much tomato juice, reduce by boiling briskly for a few minutes.

VARIATION:
100 g/4 oz button mushrooms may be added to the ratatouille.
KJ/calorie count: 500/120

Top: Mushrooms à la grecque
Centre: Courgettes lyonnaise
Bottom: Ratatouille

VEGETABLE SOUFFLÉS

Swedes, spinach and leeks are excellent vegetables to use in a soufflé for a main course or starter. About 350 g/12 oz cooked and mashed vegetable is sufficient for a soufflé serving four. There are two ways to prepare vegetable soufflés and the second method produces a more substantial dish.

METHOD I

Preparation time: 15 minutes
Cooking time: 50 minutes
KJ/calorie count: swedes and leeks –
  965/240; spinach – 960/230

25 g/1 oz butter
25 g/1 oz plain flour
450 ml/¾ pint skimmed milk
6 eggs, separated
350 g/12 oz mashed cooked
  vegetables
salt
freshly ground black pepper

1. Melt the butter in a saucepan and stir in the flour. Cook for 2 minutes, stirring.
2. Gradually add enough milk to make a fairly thick sauce.
3. Remove from the heat and beat in the egg yolks, one at a time. Add the mashed vegetables and salt and pepper.
4. Beat the egg whites until stiff and fold into the vegetable mixture.
5. Transfer to a heated 1.2 litre/2 pint soufflé dish and bake in a preheated oven at 200°C, 400°F, Gas Mark 6 for about 45 minutes until risen and golden brown. (If preferred, cook the soufflé mixture in cocotte dishes for 10-15 minutes.) Serve at once.

METHOD 2

Preparation time: 15 minutes
Cooking time: 45 minutes
KJ/calorie count: about 1130/270

8 slices bread
450 ml/¾ pint skimmed milk
6 eggs, separated
350 g/12 oz mashed cooked
  vegetables
salt
freshly ground black pepper

1. Break the bread into pieces and place in a saucepan with the milk. Simmer gently until fluffy.
2. Remove from the heat and beat in the egg yolks, one at a time. Add the mashed vegetables and salt and pepper.
3. Beat the egg whites until stiff and fold into the vegetable mixture.
4. Transfer to a heated 1.2 litre/2 pint soufflé dish and bake in a preheated oven at 200°C, 400°F, Gas Mark 6 for about 40 minutes until risen and golden brown. (If preferred, cook the soufflé mixture in cocotte dishes for 10-15 minutes.) Serve at once.

LEEKS AU GRATIN

Preparation time: 5 minutes
Cooking time: about 25 minutes
KJ/calorie count: 1460/350

8 medium leeks (about 1 kg/2 lb),
  trimmed
salt
25 g/1 oz butter
25 g/1 oz plain flour
150 ml/¼ pint skimmed milk
pinch of grated nutmeg
175 g/6 oz cheese, grated
salt
freshly ground black pepper
50 g/2 oz fresh breadcrumbs

1. Remove most of the top green leaves from the leeks.
2. Place the leeks in a saucepan of boiling salted water and cook for 15-20 minutes until tender, depending on thickness.
3. Drain, reserving the cooking liquid, and put the leeks into a flameproof serving dish. Keep hot.
4. Melt the butter in a saucepan and stir in the flour. Cook for 2 minutes, stirring.
5. Gradually add the milk and enough leek cooking liquid to make a medium thick sauce.
6. Add the nutmeg and 100 g/4 oz of the cheese and stir until melted. Add salt and pepper to taste. Pour the sauce over the leeks.

7. Mix the remaining cheese with the breadcrumbs and sprinkle over the top.
8. Place under a preheated hot grill for a few minutes until the top is golden brown.

VARIATION:
Use canned or fresh celery hearts instead of leeks, omitting the nutmeg. Fresh celery will require about 30 minutes cooking.
KJ/calorie count: 520/125 per 6 oz/175 g portion

Top back: **Vegetable soufflé**
Top left: **Baked beetroot with yogurt**
Top right: **Mushroom and cheese savoury**
Right: **Leeks au gratin**
Far right: **Spiced red cabbage**

BAKED BEETROOT WITH YOGURT

Preparation time: 10 minutes
Cooking time: 10 minutes
KJ/calorie count: 630/150

---

4 medium beetroots, cooked,
   skinned and grated
salt
freshly ground black pepper
1 teaspoon dry mustard
300 ml/½ pint plain unsweetened
   yogurt

1. Mix the grated beetroot with salt, pepper, mustard and half the yogurt. Place in a wide, shallow dish and pour the rest of the yogurt on top.
2. Bake in a preheated oven at 200°C, 400°F, Gas Mark 6 for about 10 minutes or until the mixture is heated through. (Do not let the yogurt reach boiling point as it will curdle.) Serve hot or cold.

MUSHROOM & CHEESE SAVOURY

Preparation time: 10 minutes
Cooking time: 25 minutes
KJ/calorie count: 840/200

---

100 g/4 oz mushrooms
600 ml/1 pint skimmed milk
100 g/4 oz Cheddar cheese, grated
3 eggs, beaten
4 large tomatoes, skinned and
   sliced
salt
freshly ground black pepper
1 bay leaf

1. If any of the mushrooms are large, slice them.
2. Beat the milk, cheese and eggs together.
3. Place the mushrooms and tomatoes in an ovenproof dish and pour over the egg and milk mixture. Add salt, pepper and the bay leaf.
4. Place in a roasting tin of hot water and bake in a preheated oven at 190°C, 375°F, Gas Mark 5 for about 25 minutes until the custard sets.

SPICED RED CABBAGE

Preparation time: 10 minutes
Cooking time: 30 minutes
KJ/calorie count: 210/50

---

1 red cabbage, trimmed and sliced
1 large cooking apple, peeled,
   cored and thickly sliced
1 onion, peeled and sliced
300 ml/½ pint wine vinegar
1 teaspoon mixed spice

This dish tastes best if cooked a day in advance, then reheated.

1. Place the cabbage in a flameproof casserole and arrange the apple and onion slices on top.
2. Add the vinegar and sprinkle over the mixed spice. Add just enough water to cover the cabbage.
3. Bring to the boil, cover and simmer for about 30 minutes. Serve hot.

PERSIAN NOODLES

*Preparation time: 10 minutes, plus
  salting*
Cooking time: 15 minutes
KJ/calorie count: 500/120

1 large aubergine, fairly thickly
  sliced
salt
1 chicken stock cube, crumbled
600 ml/1 pint water
100 g/4 oz tagliatelle or spaghetti
1 teaspoon mace
4 courgettes, sliced
freshly ground black pepper

1. Place the aubergine slices in a colander,
sprinkle with salt and leave for 30 minutes.
2. Rinse and dry the aubergine and chop
into bite-sized pieces.
3. Dissolve the stock cube in the water
and bring to the boil in a saucepan. Add
the noodles, and after a few minutes add
the aubergine, mace, courgettes and
pepper to taste.
4. Continue cooking for about 15 minutes
or until the noodles and vegetables are just
cooked. Taste and adjust the seasoning.

VEGETABLE CURRY

Preparation time: 15 minutes
Cooking time: about 25 minutes
KJ/calorie count: 500/120

1 small cauliflower, trimmed
8 carrots, scraped and sliced
salt
2 onions, peeled and sliced
2 large or 4 small parsnips, peeled
  and sliced
4 tomatoes, skinned and quartered
1½ tablespoons curry paste
1 chicken stock cube, crumbled
2 teaspoons low-calorie lime juice

1. Divide the cauliflower into florets.
2. Place the cauliflower and carrots in a
saucepan of boiling salted water.
3. After 10 minutes cooking, add the
onions, parsnips, tomatoes, curry paste
and stock cube.
4. Cover and cook for about 15 minutes
until all the vegetables are tender. Stir in
the lime juice.

BAKED WHITE CABBAGE & APPLES

Preparation time: 15 minutes
Cooking time: about 45 minutes
KJ/calorie count: 480/115

1 small white cabbage, finely
  shredded
3 large Granny Smith apples,
  peeled and grated
150 ml/¼ pint unsweetened
  grapefruit juice
150 ml/¼ pint plain unsweetened
  yogurt
salt
freshly ground black pepper

1. Place the cabbage and apple in layers in
a baking dish.
2. Pour over the grapefruit juice, cover
and place in a preheated oven at 200°C,
400°F, Gas Mark 6 for about 30 minutes.
3. Season the yogurt with salt and pepper.
Uncover the baking dish, pour in the
yogurt and stir well.
4. Reduce the oven temperature to 180°C,
350°F, Gas Mark 4 and continue cooking
for 10-15 minutes.

SPICED CARROT & YOGURT PURÉE

Preparation time: 15 minutes
Cooking time: 35 minutes
KJ/calorie count: 330/80

750 g/1½ lb carrots, scraped and
  sliced
salt
250 ml/8 fl oz plain unsweetened
  yogurt
pinch of mace
freshly ground black pepper

1. Place the carrots in a saucepan of
boiling salted water and simmer for about
15 minutes until tender.
2. Drain, reserving the cooking liquid.
Blend the carrots to a purée in a liquidizer
with the yogurt, or rub through a sieve.
Add a little carrot cooking liquid if
necessary.
3. Return the mixture to the rinsed out
pan and stir in the mace and salt and
pepper to taste. Reheat carefully and serve.

Top left: Persian noodles
Top right: Vegetable curry
Bottom left: Baked white
cabbage and apples
Centre: Spiced carrot and
yogurt purée
Right: Artichoke purée

ARTICHOKE PURÉE

Preparation time: 15 minutes
Cooking time: 25 minutes
KJ/calorie count: 170/40

450 g/1 lb Jerusalem artichokes,
 peeled and thickly sliced
salt
1 teaspoon wine vinegar
1 tablespoon skimmed milk powder
freshly ground black pepper
pinch of grated nutmeg (optional)

1. Place the artichokes in a saucepan of boiling salted water with the vinegar added. Simmer for about 20 minutes until tender.
2. Drain, reserving the cooking liquid, and allow to cool slightly.
3. Blend the artichokes to a purée in a liquidizer with 1 tablespoon of the cooking liquid. Add a little more liquid if necessary. Alternatively, rub through a sieve.

3. Add the skimmed milk powder, salt and pepper to taste and nutmeg, if used. Blend again until smooth.
4. Return to the saucepan and dry off the purée slightly, stirring continuously.
5. Serve with grilled steaks or lamb chops.

VARIATION:
Use parsnips instead of artichokes.
KJ/calorie count: 420/100

PUDDINGS & CAKES

CHEESECAKE

Preparation time: 25 minutes, plus setting
Cooking time: 5 minutes
KJ/calorie count: 6270/1500 for whole cake

8 digestive biscuits
40 g/1½ oz soft (tub) margarine
3 tablespoons water
350 g/12 oz curd cheese
150 ml/¼ pint plain unsweetened yogurt
3 tablespoons lemon juice
20 artificial sweetener tablets, crushed
grated rind of 2 lemons
2 eggs, separated
15 g/½ oz powdered gelatine
3 tablespoons water

1. Place the digestive biscuits in a polythene bag and crush with a rolling pin.
2. Put the margarine in a blender with the water and liquidize until the water is absorbed. From time to time stop the machine and scrape the mixture down the sides and from the blades.
3. When the water has been absorbed (shake off any excess water), mix the margarine with the biscuit crumbs. Press the mixture lightly on to the base of a lightly greased 18 cm/7 inch cake tin with a removable bottom.
4. Bake in a preheated oven at 190°C, 375°F, Gas Mark 5 for 5 minutes. Leave to cool.
5. Meanwhile, mix the curd cheese, yogurt, lemon juice and artificial sweetener tablets together. Add the lemon rind.
6. Beat the egg yolks into the mixture, one by one.
7. Sprinkle the gelatine over the water in a teacup, stand in a bowl of hot water and stir until dissolved. Add to the cheese mixture. Refrigerate for about 1 hour.
8. When the mixture thickens, whisk the egg whites until they form peaks and fold carefully into the cheese mixture.
9. Shake any surplus crumbs from the cheesecake base and then add the mixture. Leave to set in the refrigerator for about 3 hours.

VARIATIONS:
The cheesecake may be decorated in any of the following ways:
3 pineapple slices, chopped and arranged round edge.
Adds 210 KJ/50 calories
75 g/3 oz grapes, halved and deseeded and arranged round edge.
Adds 190 KJ/45 calories
100 g/4 oz strawberries, hulled, sliced and arranged round edge.
Adds 125 KJ/30 calories
Use orange rind and juice instead of lemon, and decorate with slices of orange.
Adds 60 KJ/15 calories

PAVLOVA

Preparation time: 15 minutes
Cooking time: about 20 minutes
KJ/calorie count: 400/95 for meringue

3 × size 1 or 2 egg whites
1 teaspoon cream of tartar
3 tablespoons skimmed milk
  powder
artificial liquid sweetener, to taste
450 g/1 lb mixed soft fruit (e.g.
  strawberries, kiwi fruit, grapes)

1. Beat the egg whites and cream of tartar until stiff. Fold in the skimmed milk powder and artificial sweetener.
2. Cover a baking sheet with foil and lightly brush with oil. Pile the mixture on to the baking sheet and then flatten into a circle with a palette knife.
3. Bake in a preheated oven at 120°C, 250°F, Gas Mark ½ for about 20 minutes. Cool and loosen carefully with the palette knife.
4. Place on a serving dish and arrange the fruit on top of the meringue.

VARIATION:
Add 2 teaspoons instant coffee powder or granules to the mixture with the skimmed milk powder. Serve with Coffee Sorbet (see page 121).

APRICOT & ALMOND DESSERT

Preparation time: 15 minutes, plus soaking and setting
KJ/calorie count: 630/150

225 g/8 oz dried apricots
1 tablespoon powdered gelatine
50 ml/2 fl oz hot water
2 tablespoons skimmed milk
  powder
artificial liquid sweetener, to taste
1 teaspoon almond or vanilla
  essence

1. Place the apricots in a bowl, add water to cover and leave to soak overnight. Drain and reserve the liquid.
2. Place the gelatine in the hot water and stir until dissolved.
3. Put the gelatine and drained apricots into a blender with the skimmed milk powder, artificial sweetener and almond or vanilla essence.
4. Add enough apricot soaking liquid to make a thick, smooth consistency when liquidized. Pour into individual glasses and leave to set.

GOOSEBERRY CHARLOTTE

Preparation time: 20 minutes
Cooking time: 30 minutes
KJ/calorie count: 630/150

750 g/1½ lb gooseberries, topped
  and tailed
a little lemon juice
artificial liquid sweetener, to taste
25 g/1 oz low-calorie spread
4 slices wholemeal bread
1 teaspoon ground cinnamon

1. Place the gooseberries in a saucepan with a little lemon juice and artificial sweetener.
2. Cover, bring to the boil and simmer for 10 minutes until the gooseberries are just softened. Transfer to an ovenproof dish.
3. Spread a little low-calorie spread on to the bread slices, cut into quarters and arrange on top of the gooseberries. Sprinkle with the cinnamon.
4. Place in a preheated oven at 200°C, 400°F, Gas Mark 6 and bake for about 20 minutes until the bread topping is browned.

SUMMER PUDDING

Serves 8
Preparation time: 20 minutes, plus setting
KJ/calorie count: 420/100

8 slices stale white bread, crusts
  removed
1 kg/2 lb stewed fruit with plenty
  of juice

The fruit used for summer pudding can vary according to availability. Try black and redcurrants, blackberry and apple, raspberries, or a mixture of soft fruit.

1. Place a slice of bread at the bottom of a pudding basin. Soak it with some of the stewed fruit juice.
2. Cut 5 slices into three and line the sides of the basin. Add the fruit and place the

remaining 2 slices of bread on top.
3. Pour the rest of the juice over the pudding. Place a plate on top and press down with a weight.
4. Leave in the refrigerator overnight. Turn out and serve.

BANANA FOOL

Preparation time: 10 minutes, plus chilling
KJ/calorie count: 355/85

2 bananas, peeled
300 ml/½ pint plain unsweetened yogurt
artificial liquid sweetener, to taste

1. Mash the bananas with a fork.
2. Beat into the yogurt, adding artificial sweetener to taste.
3. When well blended, spoon the mixture into individual dishes and chill before serving.

VARIATIONS:
Use 225 g/8 oz puréed strawberries or raspberries or finely chopped fresh or canned (in unsweetened juice) pineapple instead of the bananas.

KJ/calorie count: strawberries 210/50, raspberries 210/50, pineapple 230/55

APPLE AMBER

Preparation time: 15 minutes
Cooking time: 10 minutes
KJ/calorie count: 420/100

4 large dessert apples, peeled, cored and sliced
lemon juice
artificial liquid sweetener, to taste
2 eggs, separated
grated nutmeg

1. Place the apple slices in a saucepan with enough lemon juice to prevent burning. Add artificial liquid sweetener to taste.
2. Cover and cook slowly until the apples are soft, adding more lemon juice if necessary.
3. Mash the apples and allow to cool.
4. Stir the egg yolks into the apple mixture.

5. Beat the egg whites until stiff and fold in. Sprinkle with nutmeg.

Top left: Pavlova
Centre: Apricot and almond dessert
Right: Apple amber
Bottom left: Gooseberry charlotte
Centre: Summer pudding
Right: Banana fool

ROSY PEARS

Preparation time: 10 minutes
Cooking time: about 30 minutes
KJ/calorie count: 420/100

4 large firm pears, peeled, cored
    and quartered
250 ml/8 fl oz orange juice
120 ml/4 fl oz red wine
20-30 cardamom seeds
artificial liquid sweetener, to taste
    (optional)

1. Place the pears in a soufflé dish and pour on the orange juice and red wine.
2. Crack each cardamom seed with the back of a spoon and add to the dish.
3. Bake in a preheated oven at 200°C, 400°F, Gas Mark 6 for about 30 minutes, depending on the hardness of the pears. When cooked, taste for sweetness and, if liked, add artificial sweetener.
4. Serve hot or chilled, with plain unsweetened yogurt. Non-slimmers can serve with cream.

ORANGE YOGURT JELLY

Preparation time: 10 minutes, plus
    setting
Cooking time: 5 minutes
KJ/calorie count: 540/130

25 g/1 oz powdered gelatine
600 ml/1 pint unsweetened orange
    juice
300 ml/½ pint plain unsweetened
    yogurt
1 orange, peeled and sliced, to
    decorate

1. Sprinkle the gelatine into the orange juice in a saucepan and leave for about 5 minutes to soften. Dissolve the gelatine by heating the mixture, stirring continuously.
2. Allow to cool slightly then whisk in the yogurt using a fork.
3. Pour into a 900 ml/1½ pint mould and leave to set. Unmould and decorate with the orange slices just before serving.

BAKED FRUIT SALAD

Preparation time: 10 minutes
Cooking time: about 20 minutes
KJ/calorie count: 500/120

1 grapefruit
2 oranges
1 eating apple, sliced – Cox's
    Orange Pippin preferably
8 dried apricot halves
300 ml/½ pint unsweetened
    orange juice

1. Slice the grapefruit and oranges, leaving on the peel.
2. Place the grapefruit, orange and apple slices in a casserole dish with the apricots. Use the ends of the oranges and grapefruit to cover the top.
3. Pour in the orange juice and cover. Bake in a preheated oven at 200°C, 400°F, Gas Mark 6 for about 20 minutes until all the fruit is soft. Serve hot or cold.

FRESH FRUIT SALAD

Preparation time: 15 minutes
KJ/calorie count: 420/100

2 dessert apples, peeled and sliced
1 banana, peeled and sliced
juice of 1 lemon
3 oranges
1 grapefruit, peeled, sliced and
    halved
100 g/4 oz grapes, deseeded
artificial liquid sweetener, to taste

1. Toss the apple and banana slices in the lemon juice to prevent discoloration.
2. Peel and slice one of the oranges and squeeze the juice from the remaining two.
3. Remove any pith and pips from the orange and grapefruit slices.
4. Add the orange, grapefruit and grapes to the apple and banana slices, and mix well.
5. Add the orange juice and a little artificial liquid sweetener to taste, if necessary.

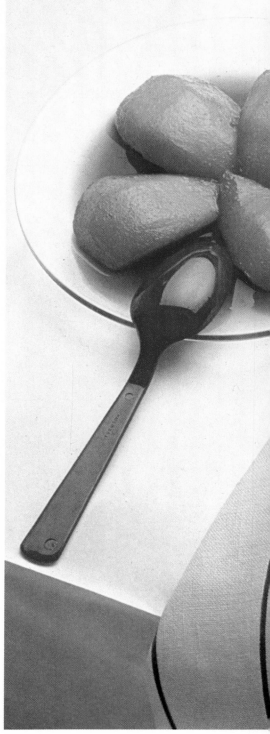

Top left: Rosy pears
Centre: Orange yogurt jelly
Top right: Grapefruit jelly
Bottom left: Baked fruit salad
Bottom right: Fresh fruit salad

GRAPEFRUIT JELLY

Preparation time: 15 minutes, plus setting
KJ/calorie count: 210/50

15 g/½ oz powdered gelatine
300 ml/½ pint hot water
300 ml/½ pint unsweetened grapefruit juice
1 grapefruit

1. Sprinkle the gelatine into the hot water and stir until dissolved.
2. Add the grapefruit juice.
3. Finely grate the rind of the grapefruit and stir into the gelatine mixture.
4. Pour into a 600 ml/1 pint jelly mould and leave to set.
5. Peel and cut the grapefruit into segments, removing the skin and pith.

Turn out the jelly and decorate with the grapefruit segments.

VARIATION:
Use half and half lemon and orange juice and 2 oranges instead of grapefruit, adding artificial liquid sweetener to taste.

FRUIT BRÛLÉE

Preparation time: 20 minutes, including making purée, plus chilling
Cooking time: 2-3 minutes
KJ/calorie count: plums: 520/125
rhubarb: 420/100
raspberries: 520/125

450 g/1 lb any soft fruit purée (e.g. plums, rhubarb, raspberries)
150 ml/5 fl oz soured cream
4 teaspoons brown sugar

1. Into the bottom of 4 ramekins put an equal quantity of fruit purée.
2. Pour an equal quantity of soured cream over the purée. Chill for at least 2 hours.
3. Sprinkle a teaspoonful of brown sugar over each dish, then place under a preheated hot grill until the sugar bubbles and turns golden brown.
4. Chill for at least 2 hours before serving.

PEACHES IN ORANGE JUICE

Preparation time: 10 minutes
Cooking time: about 20 minutes
KJ/calorie count: 330/80

4 × 175 g/6 oz ripe peaches, skinned
250 ml/8 fl oz unsweetened orange juice

1. Cut the peaches in half and remove the stones.
2. Place in a soufflé dish and pour the orange juice over. Cook in a preheated oven at 180°C, 350°F, Gas Mark 4 for 20 minutes or until tender.
3. Serve hot or cold. Non-slimmers can serve this with cream and brown sugar.

COFFEE SORBET

Preparation time: 10 minutes, plus freezing
KJ/calorie count: 480/115

600 ml/1 pint plain unsweetened yogurt
4 tablespoons skimmed milk powder
4 teaspoons instant coffee powder or granules
artificial liquid sweetener, to taste

1. Mix the yogurt, skimmed milk powder and instant coffee together. Add artificial sweetener to taste and stir well.
2. Pour into a shallow dish and place in the freezing compartment of the refrigerator for 3-4 hours.
3. Stir occasionally, mixing the frozen edges to the centre. Do not allow the sorbet to freeze hard as the mixture should be soft.
4. Non-slimmers can serve this with cream.

PEACH SORBET

Preparation time: 10 minutes, plus freezing
KJ/calorie count: 420/100

450 g/1 lb canned peaches, weighed without juice
2 tablespoons unsweetened orange juice
2 tablespoons skimmed milk powder
artificial liquid sweetener, to taste (optional)

It is important to use only peaches which have been canned in unsweetened peach juice or unsweetened apple juice.

1. Place the peaches, orange juice, skimmed milk powder and artificial sweetener, if using, into a blender and liquidize until smooth.
2. Spoon into a shallow dish and place in the freezer compartment of the refrigerator for 3-4 hours.
3. Stir occasionally, mixing the frozen edges to the centre. Do not allow the sorbet to freeze hard as the mixture should be softish and creamy.

Top left: Fruit brûlée
Top right: Peaches in orange juice
Left: Coffee sorbet
Right: Peach sorbet

CARROT CAKE

Preparation time: 20 minutes
Cooking time: about 1 hour
KJ/calorie count: 6140/1470 for whole cake

175 g/6 oz plain flour
1½ teaspoons baking powder
½ teaspoon grated nutmeg
½ teaspoon mixed spice
100 g/4 oz low-calorie spread
1 egg
100 g/4 oz caster sugar
1 small eating apple
75 g/3 oz grated carrot
2 egg whites

1. Lightly grease a 450 g/1lb loaf tin and line the base with greased greaseproof paper.
2. Sift the flour, baking powder, nutmeg and mixed spice into a mixing bowl. Add the low-calorie spread, egg and sugar. Beat together until thoroughly mixed.
3. Grate the apple into the mixture. Squeeze the juice from the carrot, then stir the grated carrot into the mixture.
4. Fold in the beaten egg whites.
5. Turn the mixture into the prepared tin and place in a preheated oven at 190°C, 375°F, Gas Mark 5 for about 1 hour or until a skewer inserted in the centre comes out clean.

CURRANT CAKE

Preparation time: 15 minutes
Cooking time: about 1 hour
KJ/calorie count: 6520/1560 for whole cake

175 g/6 oz self-raising flour
1 teaspoon baking powder
½ teaspoon mixed spice
100 g/4 oz low-calorie spread
100 g/4 oz caster sugar
1 egg
50 g/2 oz currants
1½ teaspoons grated orange rind
2 egg whites, stiffly beaten

1. Lightly grease a 450 g/1 lb loaf tin and line the base with greased greaseproof paper.
2. Sift the flour, baking powder and mixed spice into a mixing bowl. Add the low-calorie spread, sugar and egg. Beat together very thoroughly, for at least 2 minutes.
3. Add the currants and grated orange rind and beat again.
4. Fold in the very stiffly beaten egg whites.
5. Turn the mixture into the prepared tin and place in a preheated oven at 190°C, 375°F, Gas Mark 5 for about 1 hour or until a skewer inserted in the centre comes out clean.

ORANGE CAKE

Preparation time: 15 minutes
Cooking time: about 1 hour
KJ/calorie count: 9950/2380 for whole cake

175 g/6 oz low-calorie spread
finely grated rind of 2 large oranges
3 tablespoons orange juice
225 g/8 oz self-raising flour
175 g/6 oz caster sugar
5 eggs, separated

1. Lightly grease a 1 kg/2 lb loaf tin and line the base with greased greaseproof paper.
2. Put the low-calorie spread, orange rind and juice, sifted flour, sugar and egg yolks into a mixing bowl and beat together until thoroughly mixed.
3. Beat the egg whites until stiff and fold into the orange mixture.
4. Turn the mixture into the prepared tin and place in a preheated oven at 190°C, 375°F, Gas Mark 5 for about 1 hour or until a skewer inserted in the centre comes out clean.

Left: Carrot cake
Centre: Orange cake
Right: Currant cake

DRINKS

PINK TONIC

Preparation time: 2 minutes
KJ/calorie count: 40/10

4 × 241 ml/8.5 fl oz splits low-
   calorie tonic water
few drops of angostura bitters
ice cubes

1. Pour the tonic water into 4 glasses and
stir a few drops of angostura bitters into
each glass.
2. Add ice and serve.

MOCK WHISKY

Preparation time: 2 minutes
KJ/calorie count: 20/5

4 × 241 ml/8.5 fl oz splits low-
    calorie ginger ale
4 tablespoons low-calorie lime
    juice
ice cubes

1. Pour the ginger ale into 4 glasses and
stir 1 tablespoon lime juice into each glass.
2. Add ice and serve.

WEST INDIAN COOLER

Preparation time: 5 minutes
KJ/calorie count: 210/50

250 ml/8 fl oz unsweetened orange
    juice
250 ml/8 fl oz unsweetened
    pineapple juice
ice cubes
soda water

1. Pour the orange and pineapple juices
equally into 4 glasses, so that they are
about half full.
2. Add ice and top up with soda water.

BANANA SHAKE

Preparation time: 5 minutes
KJ/calorie count: 520/125

2 bananas, peeled
1.2 litres/2 pints skimmed milk
4 ice cubes
artificial liquid sweetener, to taste

1. Place all the ingredients except the
sweetener in a blender.
2. Liquidize until smooth. Add artificial
liquid sweetener to taste.
3. Serve in tall glasses.

ORANGE YOGURT SHAKE

Preparation time: 5 minutes
KJ/calorie count: 310/75

600 ml/1 pint unsweetened orange
    juice
300 ml/½ pint plain unsweetened
    yogurt
4 ice cubes
artificial liquid sweetener, to taste

1. Place all the ingredients except the
sweetener in a blender.
2. Liquidize until smooth. Add artificial
liquid sweetener to taste.
3. Serve in tall glasses.

VARIATION:
Grapefruit, low-calorie lime juice or lemon
juice can be used instead of orange juice.

MOCHA SHAKE

Preparation time: 5 minutes
KJ/calorie count: 420/100

25 g/1 oz cocoa powder
1.2 litres/2 pints skimmed milk
2 teaspoons instant coffee powder
    or granules
4 ice cubes
artificial liquid sweetener, to taste

1. Place all the ingredients except the
sweetener in a blender.
2. Liquidize until smooth. Add artificial
liquid sweetener to taste.
3. Serve in tall glasses.

**Left to right: Pink tonic; Mock
whisky; West Indian cooler;
Banana shake; Orange yogurt
shake; Mocha shake**

INDEX

INDEX